THE SOUT
ENGLAND

EXPLORING WOODLAND

WOODLAND
TRUST

THE SOUTH EAST OF ENGLAND

Edited by Graham Blight

F

FRANCES LINCOLN LIMITED
PUBLISHERS

Acknowledgements

Introduction by Archie Miles
Site entries written by Sheila Ashton
Researched by Sarah Underhill & Janet Watt
Edited by Graham Blight
Maps by Linda M Dawes, Belvoir Cartographics & Design
Regional maps created using Maps in Minutes data © MAPS IN MINUTES™ 2004.
© Crown Copyright, Ordnance Survey 2004
Site maps © Woodland Trust 2006

Photographic acknowledgements

Chris Yarrow: 94; Christopher Kemp: 19, 123; Graham Dennis: 23, 24
National Trust: 17, 31, 59, 60, 62, 79
Natural Image/Bob Gibbons: 1, 37, 38; Stephen Robson: 2
Stuart Handley/Foto45: 15, 29, 34, 83, 84, 87, 88, 100, 102, 103, 104
Sussex Wildlife Trust: 50, 52
Woodland Trust: 8, 11, 26, 40, 45, 55, 67 (Roy Battell), 71, 76, 80 (Roy Battell), 81 (Roy Battell), 85, 95 (Mike Brown), 97, 106 (Kenneth Watkins), 108, 111, 112, 114, 115, 116 (Pete Holmes), 120, 121

Frances Lincoln Ltd
4 Torriano Mews
Torriano Avenue
London NW5 2RZ
www.franceslincoln.com

The South East of England
Copyright © Frances Lincoln 2006
Text © Woodland Trust 2006
Maps © see above

First Frances Lincoln edition: 2006

A catalogue record for this book is available from the British Library.

ISBN 10: 0-7112-2659-8
ISBN 13: 978-0-7112-2659-3

Printed and bound in Singapore
The paper used in this book was sourced from sustainable forests, managed according to FSC (Forest Stewardship Council) guidelines.

1 2 3 4 5 6 7 8 9

Half title page New Forest
Title page Mens Nature Reserve

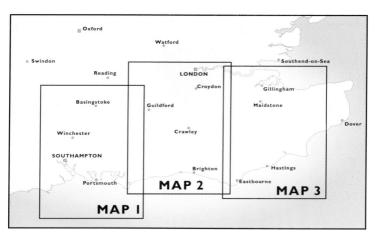

Contents

How to use this guide

Covering a region that encompasses Kent, Surrey, Sussex, Hampshire, the Isle of Wight and South London, this book is divided into three areas represented by key maps on pages 18, 46 and 90. The tree symbols on these maps denote the location of each wood. In the pages following the key maps, the sites nearest one another are described together (wherever practical) to make planning a day out as rewarding as possible.

For each site entry the name of the nearest town/village is given, followed by road directions and the grid reference of the site entrance. The area of the site (in hectares followed by acres) is given together with the official status of the site where appropriate and the owner, body or organisation responsible for maintaining the site. Symbols are used to denote information about the site and its facilities as explained in the next column.

Type of wood

Mainly broadleaved woodland

Mainly coniferous woodland

Mixed woodland

Car park

Parking on site

Parking nearby

Parking difficult to find

Official status

Area of Outstanding Natural Beauty AONB

Site of Special Scientific Interest SSSI

Site facilities

Sign at entry

Information board

One or more paths suitable for wheelchair users

Dogs allowed under supervision

Waymarked trail

Toilet

Picnic area

Entrance/car park charge

Refreshments on site

The South East of England

Joydens Wood

Pounding relentlessly round the M25, the nose-to-tail traffic hurtles day and night, seemingly a world away from the pastoral delights of the Kent and Surrey countryside and its remarkable array of beautiful and diverse woodlands; and yet many are but a short step from this frantic tarmac treadmill. If ever a part of Britain needed the peaceful havens of its woodlands then surely it is here.

Looking at the map, the first impression of southeast England is one of a densely populated area with its associated road and rail network and yet, in spite of this, much of Kent, Sussex and Surrey, collectively known as the Weald, forms one of the most heavily wooded areas of Britain. This status has endured throughout recorded history largely because the coppiced wood and larger timber were more important to the region's economy than the alternative use of the land for agriculture. In recent history the infamous gales of 1987 did their utmost to destroy much of these woods, but even in the face of such extreme elements their vibrancy could not be quashed. Replanting and a great deal of natural regeneration has already healed most of the scars.

The splendid botanic gardens at Kew weren't spared the devastation of the gales either. However, it's a great tribute to the staff that Kew Gardens look as peerless as ever today. Not perhaps everyone's idea of woodland, Kew does have many stands of different types of trees along with its splendid collection of individual specimen trees from around the world. This is a great place either to begin your acquaintance with trees or to broaden your knowledge; taking advantage of the 250 years of expertise, enthusiasm and commitment which have created one of the finest collections of trees and plants in the world. One of Kew's most special trees is the 'Old Lion' ginkgo biloba – a so-called fossil tree, which is a direct descendant from the ginkgo family of 200 million years ago – once growing worldwide, but with a native range now confined to a mountainous region of southeast China. Its form has remained virtually unchanged to this day, as fossil remains found in northeast England testify. This is just one star out of many, but the importance of Kew is that this is the place to really get to grips with positively identifying trees (helpfully, they're all labeled), so that when you encounter some of the introduced or exotic species elsewhere you'll know exactly what you're looking at.

With such a large and diverse selection of woodlands to visit in the southeast it's impossible to mention most of them here, but a sampling of different types should whet the appetite for woodland adventuring.

Many of the larger open spaces with woodland in southern suburban London and northern Surrey are old parkland or commons, and all these sites have their own specific merits. Ashtead Common is most famous for its 2,000 ancient oak pollards, remnants of an old wood pasture regime. Some of the trees will be 300-400 years old and their gnarled old forms have become havens for all manner of birdlife, bats and bugs. If you're jumpy about creepy-crawlies you might not like to know that 1,000 species of beetles have been found here – 150 being internationally rare. Londoners treasure these green spaces as somewhere close at hand to walk the dog, let the kids go wild, ride bikes or horses or just sit to chill out. Wimbledon and Putney Commons offer bags of room for all this with woods predominantly oak/birch and beech/hornbeam, as well as heathland and ponds all linked by a network of paths and tracks. And the bonus for your healthy exertions? Excellent tea rooms (by all accounts), and they're open 363 days a year!

Head east around the old South Circular, towards Dartford, to find the fascinating wood around the remains of Lesnes Abbey, near Belvedere, where archaeology, paleontology, splendid wild flowers, a weird tree face ('Sleeping Dryad' in an old sweet chestnut), and even ring-necked parakeets are some of the treats in store – you'd be hard put to get such an eclectic mix anywhere else. Incidentally, the author is slightly relieved to know that there are other people who see faces in trees too!

At Trosley Country Park, near Meopham, you'll discover some of the most splendid views from the crest of the North Downs out across the Weald of Kent, surrounded by a superb display of wild flowers so typically associated with chalk grassland, and some thumping great yews, a lime-loving tree which pops up frequently along the chalky uplands of the whole region. Perhaps the most glorious woodland system in east Kent is that to be found around the city of Canterbury; the northwestern part being known as The Blean. At over 1,200 acres this is one of the largest broadleaved nature reserves in the whole of Britain and is comprised of a number of different habitat types, including ancient woodland, conifer plantations, heathland and sweet chestnut coppice. It is managed by a consortium of local authorities and conservation groups. Although there are some marvellous oaks and beeches here, it's the sweet chestnut which plays the pivotal role. Chestnut coppice has been the economic mainstay of these woods, probably since Roman times, for they almost certainly introduced the tree to Britain. More recently it was cut for hop poles in the nineteenth and early twentieth centuries, whilst smaller cleft pales were used for countless miles of Chestnut palings (or spiles). H.L. Edlin

Sweet Chestnuts

delivered the amazing statistic in the 1940s that, '*a skilled cleaver can make a mile of fencing, using some 25,000 pales, from an acre of chestnut coppice.*' Management of these woods has been the salvation of the heath fritillary, a nationally rare butterfly, which thrives along the open rides and glades, where it finds its main food plant, cow-wheat. For bird lovers this is the place to be if you want to catch sight or sound of the elusive nightingale and nightjar.

On the Kent/Sussex border, near Goudhurst, lies Bedgebury Pinetum – one of the world's finest conifer collections. At the last count 6,241 magnificent trees, including many rare and endangered species, grow amongst landscaped lakes and valleys. Established as the National Conifer Collection in 1925, it was the passion and energy of William Dallimore, a botanist/gardener who retired from Kew in 1936, which made the greatest impact at Bedgebury. For nine years he planted trees to complement the existing scheme established by Viscount Marshall Beresford, and an ongoing sense of scale and design has culminated in a truly superb conifer experience. Whether it be enchanting wintry landscapes in the grip of sparkling hoar frost, the organised and entertaining fungus forays of autumn to seek out some of the 975 varieties identified so far, or lazy summer days relaxing by the lakes and streams and being occasionally buzzed by some of the 19 species of dragonflies, there's always something different going on here. You can even discover Kent's tallest tree – The Old Man of Kent is a whopping great Silver fir planted in 1847 and now a staggering 163 feet high.

Once upon a time in Sussex there was a forest where a small boy and his animal friends had marvellous adventures, and eventually their story was told to the whole world. Ashdown Forest might not look like the hundred acre wood of the storybooks, for it is forest in the legal sense - a preserve where the king (or landowner) would hunt his deer at his leisure. Ironically it was the excessive numbers of deer plus the overgrazing of livestock by the commoners, which denuded much of Ashdown of its trees. Certainly there must once have been respectable amounts of coppice woodland here, since the forest was at the hub of a vibrant iron industry from the Roman occupation through to the end of the eighteenth century, and copious quantities of wood were needed to make the charcoal to fire the furnaces to smelt the iron ore. All that's left today is plenty of colonizing birch, some good stands of pine and an abundance of heathland (one of Britain's fastest disappearing habitats). The big attraction of Ashdown for many is its association with A. A. Milne's Christopher Robin and his animal friends; and it is, after all, great fun to visit The Enchanted Place (Gill's Lap) or play Pooh Sticks from the actual bridge that E. H. Shepherd drew.

Not far from Uckfield a different kind of woodland story unfolds, and one from which not only pleasure can be taken, but also a hugely informative experience encompassing the socio-economic value of woodlands both now and in the past. Wilderness Wood is managed by its resident owners as a working wood; growing sweet chestnut, pine and beech, which are harvested and converted into wood products on site. In addition every effort has been made to work in close harmony with the wildlife as well as providing educational and recreational facilities for visitors. There are frequent special events and demonstrations throughout the year, and just before Christmas you can even go and cut or dig your very own Christmas tree. The all round excellence of this woodland and the Yarrow Family who run it so enthusiastically has led to several prestigious awards in recent years.

In stark contrast to the active management at Wilderness it's interesting to take stock of a real wilderness and the way that lack of management shapes woodland. Near Petworth is an ancient common, largely composed of wood-pasture, called The Mens. Grazing of livestock ceased here a long time ago, so that much of the old pasture slowly evolved into woodland. Amongst the younger woodland trees huge old oak pollards and towering beeches interspersed by medieval wood banks and flower rich meadows form a delicious tract of landscape history which has survived almost unchanged for centuries. The name may seem strange, but it apparently derives from the Anglo-Saxon 'ge-maennes', meaning 'common land'. This is a wonderful untamed space which will hopefully remain so in the safe hands of Sussex Wildlife Trust.

The rich tapestry of our nation's history is well woven into so many of the southeastern woodlands, manifesting in all kinds of evidence of ownership, occupation and woodmanship. Take Moat Wood, for example, near East Hoathly, containing (obviously) a moat. Research has revealed that this probably dates from the thirteenth century and that a homestead with several associated farm buildings once stood upon the island it surrounds; the moat itself being more a status symbol than a defence, and quite handy as a ready source of fresh fish for the table. The woodland at Oldbury Hill (near Sevenoaks) is topped by a massive Iron Age hillfort, whilst at Joydens Wood (near Dartford) there are remains of two Iron age roundhouses, and an ancient bank and ditch (Faesten Dic) strikes through the wood. Wherever you go there are signs of the past if you can only tune into them. Watch for ancient drove roads, iron workings, charcoal hearths, saw-pits, hammer ponds and quarries. If you see things you don't understand, try and find out more; for when you understand the structure and evolution of woodlands it brings a whole new dimension to your visits.

Sometimes a woodland experience can be of awesome proportions, and perhaps few more so than a remarkable place set in the chalk downs a little way north of Chichester. If you can, go to Kingley Vale early on a misty morning, before the rest of the world is up and about. Tread cautiously into the dark depths of this ancient yew wood, keeping a watchful eye on the massive arachnoid trees, many at least 500 years old, as they crouch menacingly in the gloom. The whole place engenders a sense of edgy wonder; a sense of being watched; a sense of smallness and insignificance. Did that one just move? If you're of a nervous disposition take a friend. The site is generally considered to be the best of its type in Europe and in 1952 it became one of Britain's first designated National Nature Reserves. In the early twentieth century W.H. Hudson was moved to write: '*One has here the sensation of being in a vast cathedral: not like that of Chichester, but older and infinitely vaster, fuller of light and gloom and mystery, and more wonderful in its associations.*'

It mustn't be forgotten that just across the Solent lies the Isle of Wight, with many interesting woodlands and some of Britain's slippiest and slidiest terrain in its south coast landslips, well worth a visit if you want to see trees literally hanging in there. Parkhurst Forest is a pleasant mixture of broadleaves and conifers and one of the largest tracts of woodland on the island, tracing its roots back to the *Domesday Book*. America Wood, near Shanklin, which is principally oak, chestnut and sycamore, is probably just as old and yet its name only dates from the 1770s (prior to that it was called Little Castle Wood). Tradition has it that oak from the wood was used to build warships sent out to fight in the American War of Independence. This brings to the fore yet another intriguing aspect of woods – unraveling the meanings behind their names. While on the island keep a watchful eye out for red squirrels.

Instead of ferrying back to the racket of city life in Portsmouth or Southampton take the more peaceful connection from Yarmouth

Ashford Hangers

to Lymington and explore the New Forest, enjoying a little of its 65,500 acres of woodland of different types and sizes, open heath, ponds, streams, bogs and grassland. This is a huge location, not only due to its size, but also because of its rich biodiversity, a landscape little changed in 1,500 years, and its superlative amenity value. The Court of Verderers looks after the interests of the commoners of the forest in conjunction with the Forestry Commission who attend to the woodland management. Now designated a National Park, this should help to assure its future.

Beech, and splendid specimens at that, may be a well-known feature of the New Forest (although the grey squirrels are doing their level best to change that), but to the northeast are the famous Hampshire beech hangers where dramatic chalky scarps are clad in towering swathes of trees; and none of these more famed than Selborne Hanger. The village, along with its surrounding countryside has found immortality since the late eighteenth century when one of Britain's most celebrated naturalist/diarists, Rev. Gilbert White, published his *Natural History of Selborne*, recording in the minutest detail the natural world he observed around his Hampshire home. Even today a visit to Selborne is redolent of White's accounts and it is an evocative perambulation up through the hanger along his zig-zag path. Sadly the ancient yew tree sentinel in front of Selborne church blew down in the 1990 gales, and although the massive bole was gently levered back into the ground, with hopes of regeneration, it still perished. Nearby Binswood is an ancient common, once part of the Wolmer Forest, still grazed by commoners' stock and characterised by craggy old oak and beech pollards as well as the many areas of flower-rich grassland. These peaceful corners of Hampshire seem a million miles from the hustle and bustle of London, but there are numerous woodland treats to be discovered a short way out of the Metropolis.

Box Hill, near Dorking, is a splendid example of a woodland type now reduced to a handful of such sites nationally. Box is a native evergreen more usually associated with historic parterres or the topiaric excesses of formal gardens, but here it sprawls most informally hither and yon across the hill. Box wood was once a supremely valuable commodity prized by wood engravers for making blocks, but this market declined significantly after the nineteenth century in the face of technological improvements in commercial printing. There are still many wood engravers today who use it, but nothing approaching the same sort of scale. It's been estimated that more than a million people visit Box Hill every year and on a hot summer's day that seems a believable statistic. But try a visit 'off peak' and enjoy a good burrow around in the mysterious box groves, and discover some fine old yews, some goodly beeches and one of the lesser known rarities on the lower slopes, large-leaved lime.

Box Hill

The view from Box Hill is pretty fine, but for perhaps the most impressive view in the whole of Surrey head over to the other side of Dorking to Leith Hill. From the top of the tower on Leith Hill, built in 1765, you stand 317 metres (1,040 feet) above sea level, and on a clear day you'll see across 13 counties. It's hard to believe that the 1987 gales wreaked such devastation throughout the Wealden landscape laid before you, and yet it's equally reassuring to realise how good nature is at setting herself to rights. Trees in particular are tenacious and resilient in the face of adversity and no matter what the elements (and sometimes humans) do to them they will be around for a few more million years yet. So, study this book, realize what a treasure house of woodland is waiting for you in southeast England, and get out there and enjoy it.

ARCHIE MILES

MAP 1

The Chase p19
Benyons Inclosure p21
Pamber Forest p22
Camberley
MAP 2 ▼ (see p46)
North Wessex Downs
A338
A34
A327
A321
Kingsclere
A339
Morgaston Wood p20
A33
4a
A331
Basingstoke
6
5
Aldershot
Andover
Whitchurch
7
Farnham
A31
A343
A303
8
Home Farm p25
A325
Alice Holt Woodland Park p28
A343
HAMPSHIRE
Alton
A30
A34
Binswood p26
Haslemere
M3
New Alresford
Selborne Common p30
A3
Liphook
Winchester
A31
Great Copse p42
(A31)
10
A272
Ashford Hangers p30
Durford Wood p27
Spearywell Woods p41
Otterbourne Park Wood p40
11
Petersfield
A272
Midhurst
Romsey
A3090
A272
Harting Down p32
Upper Barn & Crowdhill Copses p39
13
Eastleigh
Queen Elizabeth Country Park p32
WEST SUSSEX
14
SOUTHAMPTON
7
A32
Sussex Downs
1
Lyndhurst
8
1
A3(M)
Stansted Forest p34
Park Wood p35
3
New Forest p36
Hythe
M27
10
Waterlooville
4
Havant
Kingley Vale p33
Fawley
11
5
A27
Chichester
Brockenhurst
Fareham
12
M275
Lymington
Gosport
Cowes
Portsmouth
Bognor Regis
Parkhurst Forest p43
Ryde
Firestone Copse p44
Selsey
Town and Walters Copse p42
Newport
Selsey Bill
Freshwater
ISLE OF WIGHT
Sandown
A3020
Borthwood Copse p44
A3055
America Wood p45
Shanklin
Ventnor

10 miles
10 km

18

The Chase
Broadlayings, Woolton Hill.

5km (3 miles) south west of Newbury on the A343. Go through Broadlaying, following brown signs to 'Rampant Cat' public house. Go past the pub and the wood is on the right, but keep going and turn right at T junction, signposted to Newbury. Car park is on right. (SU442630)

56 ha (138 acres)

National Trust

Easy on the eye – and the legs – The Chase is a wood packed with variety – conifers and broadleaves, young and mature trees, dry open areas and wet woodland with formal and informal paths.

Although there is no map or waymarked trail there is a clear path and it is not too difficult to find your way around.

Along the way you encounter all manner of trees from conifers to sweet chestnut. Follow a gravel track to the edge of open meadow where stands a magnificent spreading beech – take a seat and enjoy the view.

Away from the main path are grassy, sunny glades – great for butterflies during spring and summer.

A huge pond with a weir and central island stands in the wood's northeast corner. The scene then changes gradually from open water through marshy, boggy areas to alder and willow woodland – wonderful for flora and fauna.

The Chase

MAP 1

Morgaston Wood
Sherborne St John

6.5km (4 miles) north of
Basingstoke. Take the A340
Aldermaston Road out of
Basingstoke. Turn right into
Morgaston Road. Roadside parking
and main National Trust car park.
(SU625572) 63 ha (156 acres)
National Trust

Morgaston Wood provides the
perfect complement to a tour
of the National Trust's
neighbouring Vyne Estate.

Change and contrast are key
features of the wood which is
quite a mixture of woodland
species, from larch, pine, poplar
and hazel to birch, alder, oak
and sycamore. Entered from
the roadside parking area on
Morgaston Road, you quickly
encounter two lovely large
beech and oak trees.

Here and there are signs of
coppicing, elsewhere there are
tall dark conifers including a
stand planted on what looks
like an old pond.

The contrast between the
rich mix of plants and shrubs
beneath the broadleaves stands
out against the bare ground
supporting the conifers.

Other points of interest
include a stream which runs
along the wood's southern
edge and the occasional seat
for rest and reflection.

There is a good variety of
paths and part of the wood has
a concrete track, which should
suit wheelchair users.

Benyons Inclosure
Mortimer West End, Silchester

The wood is on the south side of
Welshman's road, the road from
Mortimer going west towards
Heath End, immediately after
Mortimer West End. Roadside
parking. (SU625640)
190 ha (470 acres)

The Englefield Estate

While this privately owned
woodland is commercially
managed for timber, there is
also an emphasis on
conservation and public access.

Scots pine is the main
species in this largely
coniferous plantation, but you
will find broadleaved trees
growing naturally along the
edges of the wide rides.

Explore the eastern edge of
the wood to discover a large,
attractive lake with water lilies.
Look for signs of a Roman
road which runs northwest to
southeast across the southern
section and, nearby, the site of
an old fort.

There is plenty to enjoy in
this area. A couple of miles
away is the Roman site of
Silchester, and, if you wish, you
can continue south again to
visit the ancient woodland of
Pamber Forest (see next page)
– a wonderful opportunity to
compare and contrast two
distinctly different woodland
characters.

The wood provides easy
walking and is enjoyed by
local people.

MAP 1

Pamber Forest

Tadley

Off A340 Basingstoke/Tadley road. Turn east at Pamber Green towards Bramley, then north to Little London and Silchester. At end of Little London, entrance is on left, opposite end of Frog Lane.
(SU625605) 191 ha (472 acres) SSSI

Hampshire & Isle of Wight Wildlife Trust

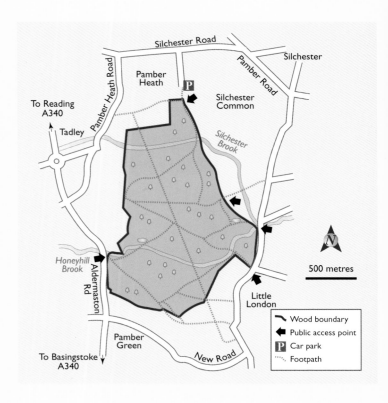

Pamber Forest

Once part of the huge Royal Forest of Windsor, Pamber Forest is a well-managed and maintained ancient woodland that provides a real feeling of peace.

A walk through Pamber leads visitors through a host of habitats, each supporting its own distinct range of wildlife, roe deer among them. The scenery changes from dry open heathland through dense hazel, chestnut stands and wood pasture, down to rich willow and alder-lined stream valleys.

On the woodland floor, particularly in the valleys, orchids can be seen growing alongside wild daffodils, primroses, violets, Solomon's seal and star of Bethlehem.

Some lovely big oaks, birch and wild service trees make up the woodland, intersected by numerous wide sunlit rides edged with butterfly-attracting plants.

More than 40 butterfly species

MAP 1

have been recorded but best of all must be the purple emperor which descends briefly from the canopy in early July. Other rare butterflies, including the small pearl-bordered fritillary and white admiral, can sometimes be glimpsed in the glades.

And the wildlife interest doesn't stop there. The ponds in summer are frenetic with darting dragonflies, several species of bat have been spotted on the wing at twilight and birdlife includes woodcock, three species of woodpecker and a variety of warblers.

Pamber was formerly used to provide timber for local crafts and industries and the traditional management of coppicing still continues. The forest today is managed both for conservation and visitors, who enjoy an extensive network of paths throughout the reserve.

You may also like to visit adjacent Silchester Common and view the remains of the Roman town of Calleva, meaning 'Woodland Town'. Pamber is all that survives of the ancient woodland that once surrounded the site. An exploration of the 1.5 miles of walls and a viewing of the amphitheatre demonstrates this was once a thriving place.

Pamber Forest

Home Farm
Burkham, Bentworth

Approx 16km (10 miles) on the A339 south of Basingstoke. On left hand side take a right turn on a bend signposted Bradley and Burkham. Right at the T–junction then sharp left after half a mile. (SU655420)

137 ha (340 acres)

Woodland Trust

Home Farm is set in a rolling landscape mosaic of farmland, woodland and hedgerows.

Visitors can witness a wood at different stages of development. Begin by wandering through areas of ancient and maturing woodland before emerging into more open spaces where young trees are beginning to establish. There is also an area of grassland creation.

The number and range of bird species visiting and nesting has increased in recent years. A number of owl and kestrel boxes were installed in 2000, and barn owls are regularly seen today.

A network of surrounding small woods and hedgerows virtually link Home Farm to oak woodland at Preston Oak Hills and Herriard Common, a planted conifer wood. These connect with other woods of substantial size in the area which provide important corridors for wildlife.

An extensive ride network, open spaces, a car park and information boards all add to the public enjoyment of this site.

MAP 1

Binswood
East Worldham

A31 to Alton. From Alton take B3004 through East Worldham, 3km (2 miles) take a right turn into a minor road (only signpost is for a bridleway). 250 metres, park at entrance to wood. (SU767377) 61 ha (151 acres) SSSI
Woodland Trust

Binswood is a random mosaic of grassland and woodland that is literally enveloped in the past. Indeed the site is practically surrounded by historic boundary banks and hedges that provide intriguing pointers to its history. The common was once part of Wolmer Forest, a royal hunting forest, and had a close association with the medieval deer park of Worldham.

Now designated a Site of Special Scientific Interest (SSSI), this is one of just a few remaining lowland woodland pastures outside the New Forest still sustained by traditional grazing of commoners' stock.

As a result it provides a glimpse of the landscape as it may well have looked in medieval times, a combination of species-rich ancient woodland, unimproved

Binswood

grassland, scrub and ancient oaks and beech trees.

One of the most striking features of the woodland is the array of fungi and lichens that cling to the veteran trees and dead wood, as well as the wealth of woodland flowers.

Durford Wood
Rogate

From the Jolly Drovers public house on the B2070 (the old A3), head east towards Rogate. Car park is 400m (0.25 mile) on the right. (SU799260)
26 ha (64 acres) AONB

National Trust

Here is a wood within a wood. Surrounded by wooded common – principally a plantation of Scots pine, Durford is an oasis of deciduous trees.

150 years ago the area would have looked quite different. The site was probably part of an extensive heath but was then planted with oak and coppiced to provide charcoal for the iron industry.

No longer coppiced, the distinctively shaped trees have developed into a fine example of sessile oak woodland which supports a variety of birds and insects. There is plenty of year-round interest starting with wood anemones and bluebells in spring through to heather glades in late summer and good autumn colour.

The National Trust is creating glades and wide tracks to ensure the heathland character is not lost.

Whilst in the area you may also like to visit nearby Forestry Commission sites at Combe Hill and Tullecombe.

MAP 1

Alice Holt Woodland Park
Farnham

Follow the A325 south from Farnham for 6.5km (4 miles). Turn left at crossroads by the Halfway House (PH). Car park is 400m (0.25mile) on the left. (SU810415)

248 ha (620 acres)

Forestry Commission

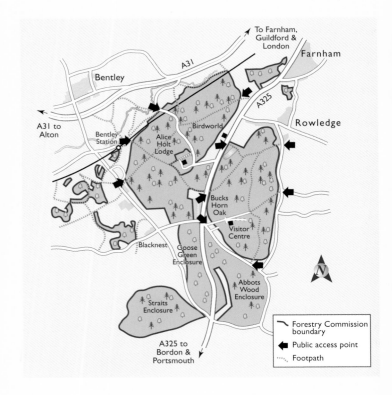

Alice Holt Woodland Park

Pack a picnic and spend a day in Alice Holt Woodland Park – the perfect place for families to enjoy a quiet walk, take a cycle ride, learn about wildlife or simply let off steam.

The site is managed not only for timber production but also has a strong emphasis on visitor enjoyment and keeping resident wildlife happy – this is truly a site with something for everyone.

The park features a wide range of amenities including a visitor centre with a shop, classroom, play areas, cycle hire, picnic areas and barbecue sites. There is also a bridlepath and a large pond within the woods.

The woodland, a mix of broadleaves and conifers, has a good mix of old and young trees and the combination of wide tracks and narrow paths beneath the closed canopy creates an interesting blend of light and shade.

Well interpreted, the site also features a habitat trail with large wooden play sculptures to discover – among them an owl, woodpecker, bat and dragonfly. You are just as likely to spy more animated wildlife, for the woods are alive with birds and butterflies, including the purple emperor.

On the other side of the A325 is a quieter, ancient woodland with its own parking, picnic areas, informal trails and paths.

This ancient forest is famous for its oaks which once supplied timber for the navy. More recently, oaks from Alice Holt were used to create the replica of Shakespeare's Globe Theatre in London.

The woodland boasts other historical links – during Roman times the site was important for pottery development and Norman kings transformed it into a royal hunting forest.

MAP 1

Ashford Hangers
Petersfield

North from Petersfield to Steep, through village and right at bottom of hill by cottage into Ashford Lane. Reserve entrance along lane, on left. (SU730265)
147 ha (363 acres) AONB SSSI
Hampshire County Council

Some of Hampshire's most beautiful, vibrant countryside awaits on the ancient and intimate swathes of steep wooded hillside known as the Hangers.

Characterised by the beech and yew of their steepest slopes, the Hangers are of international importance for their ecology.

Beneath the heavy shade of beech and yew few plants survive but out in the open glades and grassy clearings a delightful variety of wild flowers includes wood spurge, purple orchid, foxglove, tutsan and deadly nightshade.

Rare and unusual species characteristic of the Hangers include sword-leaved helleborines and herb paris. Various fungi, insects, rare molluscs and nesting birds also thrive here along with roe deer, badgers and foxes.

Surviving downland areas on the slopes boast a wealth of flora including thyme, rock rose, cowslip and eyebright. Discover the best of them at Wheatham Hill and Shoulder of Mutton Hill.

Hampshire County Council has devised a 21-mile linear path running south from Alton Railway Station through the Hangers to the South Downs at Queen Elizabeth Country Park (see p32).

Selborne Common
Alton

6.5km (4 miles) south of Alton between Selborne and Newton Valence, west of B3006. Zig-zag path and woods are a short walk from car park in village (adjacent to the Selborne Arms)
(SU742335) 98 ha (242 acres)
AONB SSSI
National Trust

One of Hampshire's renowned hangers (or wooded slopes) can be found near the village of Selborne.

Selborne Common

Hangers such as this are acclaimed as some of the richest woodland on English chalk and Selborne's is particularly important for helleborines as well as hellebores.

Beautiful beech trees – providing light in spring and colour in autumn – dominate the hanger but there is a lot more to discover. Half the common is made up of remnant wood pasture with ancient beech pollards. This area is of great ecological and landscape importance. In the area known as High Wood look for evidence of former coppicing.

A zig-zag path leads up the steep hill to the common. At the top is a wishing stone with a seat nearby and from here you can enjoy excellent views over the village and surrounding countryside.

The common is served by paths to Newton Valence and Selborne village.

MAP 1

Queen Elizabeth Country Park
Petersfield
Signed on A3, just south of
Petersfield. (SU717182)
566 ha (1400 acres) AONB SSSI
**Forestry Commission/
Hampshire County Council**

There is so much to see at
Queen Elizabeth Country Park
it is not surprising visitors
flock here. However, you can
still escape the crowds on this
rambling, beautiful site.

Dominated by the three hills
of Butser, War Down and Holt
Down, the park combines
beautiful woodland, good
visitor and children's facilities
and recreation opportunities.

Part of the forest has been
designated a Scheduled
Ancient Monument due to its
Iron Age and Roman remains.

Graded waymarked trails
through beautiful, scenic
beech woods and areas of
established conifer plantation
offer a range of opportunities
for a woodland stroll or a
horse or bike ride. West of the
A3 is Butser Hill, popular
with hang-gliders and
paragliders, with dramatic
open downland, yew woods
and mixed woodland.

Some 38 butterfly and 12
orchid species have been
recorded in the park. The
visitor centre, with its displays,
audio-visual theatre, education
and busy events programme is
a mine of information.

Harting Down
South Harting
Entrance to car park is adjacent to
the B2141, approximately 1.6km
(1 mile) south of South Harting
village. (SU790180)
240 ha (593 acres) AONB SSSI
National Trust

Popular without feeling
crowded, Harting Down Local
Nature Reserve has been
important to man for the last
5,000 years.

A hill fort, dating back to the
Iron Age, provides the most
obvious signs of a long history
but today the incredible
diversity of the site and the
exceptional views it provides
over the Weald illustrate the

importance of the woodland to the local landscape.

Remnants of the downland that was once widespread in this area can be found here, along with mature beech, yew and ash woodland and scrub with numerous flowers that draw birds and butterflies.

There is no circular waymarked trail on the site but it is possible to tackle a DIY circular route using public and permissive paths taking in the varied habitats. There are some very peaceful, sheltered walks in the cross ridge dykes. From here you can gaze over the scrub on the slopes of Round Down to the mature woodland in the south which is particularly scenic in autumn.

Kingley Vale
West Stoke

Turn west off A286 in Mid Lavant (just north of Chichester) toward West Stoke and through village. On sharp left hand bend take right turn. Car park on right. (SU824088) 150 ha (371 acres) AONB SSSI

English Nature

If you are looking for a different day out, visit Kingley Vale, a fantastic site featuring Britain's finest yew forest.

Though steep in parts, there is a rewarding climb to the top of Box Hill where you can enjoy outstanding panoramic views.

Atmospheric yew woods with some massive old trees dominate the valley slopes. The largest lie at the foot of the valley and their size and dark, contorted shapes add weight to legends of hauntings.

Near the centre of this National Nature Reserve is a yew sculpture representing 'the spirit of Kingley Vale'. You may also discover Bronze Age and Roman earthworks and barrows called the 'Devil's humps' which add archaeological interest.

Signs of roe and fallow deer, stoats, foxes, dormice and badgers can be seen. A host of tree and shrub species support thriving bird populations that include nightingale and green woodpecker while areas of open chalk grassland attract a colourful array of butterflies.

MAP 1

Stansted Forest
Rowlands Castle

From Rowlands Castle, take
Woodberry Lane southeast for
2.5km (1.5miles); then left and left
again. Forest car park is 1.6km
(1 mile) north on left. (SU753105)
485 ha (1199 acres)

Stansted Park Foundation

Peaceful and gracious, award-
winning Stansted Forest
features the longest beech
avenue planted on private land
in England and boasts some
wonderful views of Stansted
House.

A site with a host of royal
connections, the forest can be
traced back to the Roman
occupation. In the 11th
century a hunting lodge was
built for the first Earl of
Arundel.

Set around the grounds of
Stansted House, the forest won
national acclaim in 1995 for its
landscape and access
improvements, environmentally
sound timber production and
benefits for wildlife.

Various types of woodland
feature alongside open
grassland, scrub, wetland and

Stansted Forest

open water. Edged by ancient woodland with huge old trees, are mixed plantations with coppice in the heart of the forest. Access is generally easy over flat rides and paths.

This cocktail of habitats nurtures birds, butterflies and some 250 species of plantlife, including 12 species of orchid.

Park Wood
Waterlooville

Just north of Waterlooville toward Horndean, on left opposite The Queens Inclosure. (SU685103)
3 ha (7 acres)
Woodland Trust

Hailed as a unique place to visit – this site, once part of an ancient royal hunting forest, emerged from a period of neglect as a site bursting with historic, ecological and social interest.

Neglected and overgrown during the 1970s and 80s, when it also fell foul of the great storm of 1987, the wood's fortunes began to change in the 1990s, with the formation of the Friends of Park Wood. Access was improved, sycamore and laurel cleared and restoration work undertaken.

Today it is an important amenity woodland, surrounded on three sides by houses and gardens. Visually appealing, it sustains more than 140 different species, including yew, oak, Scots pine, lime, beech, holly and sycamore.

Bird and bat boxes abound on the mainly flat site and visitors of all abilities explore an impressive mix of habitats from a well-maintained network of paths. There are fine veteran trees, naturally regenerating native broadleaves, open areas and a meadow.

MAP 1

New Forest
Lyndhurst

Between Southampton, Ringwood and Lymington. Nearest rail station
at Brockenhurst. (SU300080)
26500 ha (65497 acres) AONB SSSI
Forestry Commission

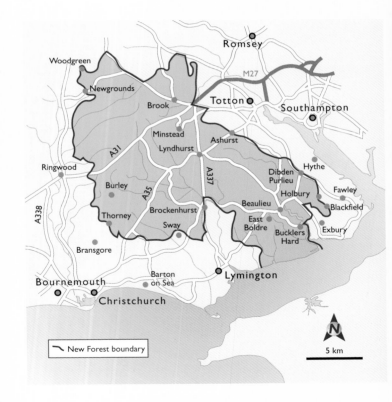

New Forest

Approached from the sea, the New Forest looks like one vast woodland interrupted by a curious mixture of heavy industry and the villas of the wealthy.

A walk across the forest reveals a much more complex landscape of wild open spaces winding around ancient farmsteads, villages and no fewer than 129 large woods.

The New Forest covers some 145 sq miles. More than 65,000 acres is woodland, with one third being enclosed plantations. The rest is pasture, open heath, bog and grassland.

Today it is criss-crossed by three busy roads and attracts a staggering seven million visitors a year. Miraculously, the landscape – looking much as it has for 1500 years – remains a unique place of remarkable peace.

MAP 1

The reason? The New Forest is a forest in the old sense, a place traditionally governed by forest law and not just of trees but incorporating swathes of heathland and forest lawn.

These exceptional pasture woods are maintained by a combination of Forestry Commission management and grazing animals owned by commoners exercising their ancient rights in the living tradition of a medieval forest. In autumn, pigs still roam to feed on acorns and beech mast. Cattle and ponies graze the woodland floor, creating a labyrinth of sunny lawns and glades.

The undoubted stars are the 'ancient and ornamental woods' where the Forestry Commission works to maintain their natural beauty, with minimal intervention.

The size of the forest and the survival of its ancient traditions support an astonishing wealth of wildlife. Even the most determined naturalist could derive a lifetime of pleasure here – and there would still be more to discover.

Located within the busy south of England, the forest is under intense pressure both from developers and for recreational use. Its recent status as a National Park brings hope that a way will be found to secure the forest's special qualities for future generations.

New Forest

Upper Barn & Crowdhill Copses
Bishopstoke

B3354 between Winchester and Botley. Sharp left turn 1.6km (1 mile) north of Fair Oak. After 100 metres turn right into Hardings Lane. Keep going to the end where there is space to park. Walk down bridleway, right turn into Crowdhill Copse. (SU484194) 28 ha (69 acres)

Woodland Trust

Once part of the Bishop of Winchester's hunting grounds, Upper Barn and Crowdhill Copses have had a chequered history.

Largely replanted in the 1950s and 60s, native broadleaves are gradually emerging to dominate the ancient woodland site, which forms an important part of the local landscape.

They lie in a rural area north of Southampton. Crowdhill Copse, in the southern part of the site, is a broad, curved belt running southeast of a small stream valley, while the larger Upper Barn Copse lies north. Both are popular with locals.

Rich in wildlife, the copses are home to 11 species of fern and many plants associated with ancient woodland – including bluebells, butcher's broom and Solomon's seal.

Close inspection reveals rich and expanding ground flora, old woodbanks and boundary trees. Buzzards and sparrow hawks can be heard, while long-tailed tits and goldcrests are common.

Access is via a good, occasionally muddy and rutted, path and ride layout.

MAP 1

Otterbourne Park Wood
Otterbourne

Junction 12 off M3 toward
Otterbourne. Turn right towards
The Otter pub. After 100 metres
turn left up lane.
(SU458222) 26 ha (64 acres)
Woodland Trust

A County Heritage site,
Otterbourne Park Wood boasts
a former Roman road running
through part of the site,
evidence of which can still be
seen.

Though steep and slippery,
this ancient woodland is well

Otterbourne Park Wood

used by nearby residents and features oak, ash, maple and wet valley alders, some of which are believed to date back to 1800.

A public footpath runs from the top of the wood and down the hill to the northeast corner.

There are large areas of regeneration where wild cherry, black poplars, rowan, sallow and hawthorns are establishing. Ground cover is dominated by bracken, bramble, holly and ivy, dotted with the typical woodland sight of yellow pimpernel, yellow archangel and moschatel. In wetter areas bugle and yellow marsh saxifrage thrive while kingcups and lesser spearwort flourish around the water.

While in the area, perhaps extend your visit to nearby Valley Park Woods in Chandlers Ford (SU424210).

Spearywell Woods
Mottisfont, Nr Romsey

Main entrance adjacent to B3084, approx 6.5km (4 miles) north of Romsey. (SU315276)
22 ha (54 acres)
National Trust

Managed for timber by the National Trust, Spearywell Woods is a peaceful, easy-to-explore mixed woodland with all the ingredients for a great family day out.

Parts of the wood date back more than 250 years though much was planted in the 1930s and this is reflected in the variety of trees. Stands of tall, elegant young beech trees lead into mixed woodland of oak, ash, birch and sweet chestnut with conifers.

Butterflies such as speckled wood and the rarer silver-washed and pearl-bordered fritillaries frequent the ride edges in these broadleaved areas. Then the mood changes with tall, pure conifer stands casting deep shadows.

The waymarked route provides a full six-mile tour of the estate but you can complete a circular walk of the wood in 45 minutes.

Spearywell Woods are part of the Mottisfont Estate which includes the ancient woodland site of Great Copse – see next entry.

MAP 1

Great Copse
Mottisfont, Nr Romsey

On the B3084 6.5km (4 miles) north
of Romsey. Right turning just north
of Spearywell Woods. Or north from
Mottisfont village, turning left after
main entrance to Abbey. (SU320282)
21 ha (52 acres)

National Trust

Great Copse is part of the
Mottisfont Estate, a 12th-
Century Augustinian priory,
which was converted into a
private house after the
dissolution of the monasteries.

Nestling in impressive
countryside along the River
Test, this ancient woodland is a
wildlife haven that teems with
flowers and butterflies – up to
20 species – in spring and
summer. Wide rides and
glades have been created to
encourage wildlife.

Look out for white admiral
butterflies in June and the rare,
silver-washed fritillary in July.
Oak standards and hazel
coppice can be found and a
host of typical ancient
woodland flowers are here to
be enjoyed – among them
bluebells, anemones, primroses,
violets, early purple orchids,
wild sorrel and the rare
Solomon's seal.

The site is small enough to
cover in an hour so a visit can
easily be combined with a tour
of the abbey and gardens,
when open, and Spearywell
Woods (see p41), also part of
the estate.

Town and Walters Copse
Porchfield

Take the A3054 Yarmouth to
Newport road. Turn left at Shalfleet
Garage towards Porchfield. After
about 800m (0.5 mile), turn left to
Newtown. Park in Newtown car
park on left, with information point.
(SZ430905) 24 ha (59 acres)

National Trust

You can feel a million miles
from civilisation on a visit to
Town and Walters Copse.

Quiet and peaceful, the
woods are managed as
traditional coppice and sustain
a wealth of wildlife including
small mammals – especially
dormice – and even the
red squirrel.

Paths are not waymarked but
it's not difficult to find your

way if you have your wits about you (note cyclists are not allowed). The path from the Town Copse entrance leads to an estuary with stunning views where you might spot oyster catcher, shelduck or redshank.

A delightful tunnel of hazel leads on past two contrasting areas, one side wild, dense and seemingly unmanaged. The other a coppiced section, where light can reach the woodland floor, breathing life into bluebells, wood anemones, wood spurge and yellow archangel. In spring, butterflies inhabit more open sections.

In contrast, Walters Copse has an airy feel with wider rides and sections of coppice.

Parkhurst Forest
Newport

Take the A3054 Newport to Yarmouth road. Main entrance is beside two wooden houses, 3km (2 miles) from Newport. (SZ480900)
395 ha (976 acres)
Forestry Commission

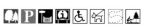

Escape to Parkhurst! – Forest, that is – for it has the feel of a big wood with cells of contrast, in the sights, sounds and even the smells the visitor can encounter.

A real assortment of conifers and broadleaves, young and old planting and dense and open areas, it has lots to discover.

The conifer stands lining the gravel track are much quieter than the broadleaved areas where you can hear the wind whistling through the leaves. Conifer needles make the ground soft and springy underfoot and their scent is striking, particularly after rain.

Keep your eyes open and you might also spot some carved faces in an old beech coppice tree as you walk along the red squirrel trail and visit the squirrel viewing hide. Routes are well waymarked, with cycling permitted on the gravel tracks, and you can take advantage of some strategically placed seats.

43

MAP 1

Firestone Copse
Wootton

Just east of Wootton bridge, turn southeast from the A3054. Follow the Firestone Copse road for 1.6km (1 mile). Car park on the right. (SZ559910)
98 ha (242 acres)
Forestry Commission

If you are exploring the area by bike, a slight detour on the Round the Island cycle route takes you through Firestone Copse where cyclists can make use of the gravel tracks.

Those exploring by foot can enjoy the Wootton Creek Trail where heron and water vole may be spotted on the water's edge while buzzards circle overhead.

Mysterious areas of dark pine forest exude wonderfully aromatic smells. At the heart of the wood, growing alongside tall pines are majestic conifers and redwoods. By contrast the sunny grassy rides are flanked by oak, ash and hazel.

Colourful flowers edge the rides providing food for butterflies such as brimstone and white admiral. Selective thinning of trees has created pockets of light in other areas of the wood.

Situated halfway between Ryde and Cowes on the north of the Island, the area is served by various transport links. The Isle of Wight Steam Railway runs just to the south.

Borthwood Copse
Apse Heath, Nr Sandown

Take the A3056 from Newport to Sandown. Turn left at Apse Heath mini roundabout and the entrance is 800m (0.5 mile) on right (Alverstone Road). (SZ567843)
24 ha (59 acres)
National Trust

A visit to Borthwood Copse brings many rewards for those armed with a good sense of direction. Find your way to the heart of the wood and you can enjoy delightful views of the white chalk of Culver Cliff.

This delightfully natural ancient woodland does provide a navigational challenge, not helped by an ageing information board which is difficult to decipher. But persevere – you will see impressive, large trees as old as 400 years.

A walk along the sometimes-muddy main path brings an early reward in the shape of two majestic beech trees and a big old oak.

In places, Borthwood is overgrown with bracken and bramble giving it a wild feel. Observant visitors might be lucky to spy red squirrels among the sweet chestnuts and hazel that dominate. The taller, more unusual sessile oak can be found here growing alongside silver birch, beech, field maple and holly.

America Wood
Shanklin
Take Apse Manor Road off A3020 just west of Shanklin. (SZ567820)
11 ha (27 acres) SSSI
Woodland Trust

It takes a bit of stamina and determination to get into America Wood, on the outskirts of Shanklin, since it has little accessible parking.

However, the more active Isle of Wight visitor can make use of public footpaths and bridleways that lead into the wood.

There is an 'open' feel to the site with storm damage in 1987 and 1990 creating lots of open sections. There is one particularly large glade which is gradually reverting to woodland.

While much is thought to be ancient woodland, the northern section has a mixture of conifers and broadleaves.

Unusually for the Isle of Wight, most of the wood today is high oak forest with downy birch.

The woodland floor supports a great deal of holly but little else in the way of ground cover. A badger sett has been reported and red squirrels occasionally spotted.

America Wood

MAP 2

Eartham Wood
Chichester

From Chichester, take the A27 east. After about 1.6km (1 mile) turn left onto the A285 to Petworth. Take the second turning to the right signed Eartham; the car park is 200m on the left. (SU936106)

260 ha (643 acres)

Forestry Commission

As public access to Eartham Wood is not widely promoted, this commercial beech site is a quiet place with a number of attractive features including pretty vistas.

A gently sloping 1.6km (1 mile) waymarked trail follows paths lined with foxgloves and later with hemp agrimony and St John's wort through the semi-mature woodland.

Pretty in the spring when light filters through the young trees, it is good too for autumn colour. And summer provides the chance to watch butterflies feed on the flowering plants in dappled sunshine.

The waymarked route passes through a young Norway spruce plantation before joining the Monarch's Way footpath, on the old Stane Street Roman road, through the beech plantation where impressive larch and large, clean-stemmed beech trees line the path.

It is worth combining your visit with a trip to nearby Selhurst Park woods which provide some fantastic views south to Halnaker Hill and the coast.

MAP 2

Slindon Woods
Slindon

On the A27 north from Chichester, take the first turning left after the Fontwell roundabout into Dukes Road. Car park is 200m along on the right. Second car park is on top of Bignor Hill. (SU952073) 550 ha (1359 acres)
National Trust

Major changes have taken place in Slindon Park's extensive woodland.

In May a sea of bluebells washes over the woods, making way for a summer shower of golden yellow broom and elegant purple foxgloves.

Once famous for towering beech trees, many of the greatest specimens were shaken by the storms of 1987 and 1990. A few survived to witness the wood develop a more diverse spread of species and see important new habitats form in dead and decaying trees.

A remnant deer park, dating back to the Middle Ages, can be found at the southern end and Iron Age field terraces, and a folly can be seen in a section known as the Nore.

More than 20 miles of paths provide access to the site which includes the ancient oak woodland of Slindon Bottom, Longbeat, a beech plantation and Black Jack. The remote and peaceful North Scarp Wood is designated a Site of Special Scientific Interest (SSSI).

Church Copse, Clapham Woods
Clapham

Turn off the A280 into Clapham village. At the cross roads turn left to Church. (TQ005067) 10 ha (25 acres) AONB
JF and CC Somerset

Part of larger Clapham Woods, Church Copse's distinctive character has been formed through continued management of hazel by coppicing. Displays of bluebells return each spring as a reward.

Coppiced wood used to be cut from Church Copse for making hurdles, which were used at nearby Findon Sheep Fair during the last century.

Dense and mystical groups of large oak trees grow alongside field maple and ash.

A range of footpaths lead visitors up and down the gentle to moderate slopes and, in one place, across a mysterious steep gully. A circular route can be enjoyed but appropriate footwear is required in winter as paths become muddy.

Do not let the absence of a sign or information board at the entrance put you off. This attractive wood is much enjoyed and used by local people. Visitors may witness coppicing in action as BTCV volunteers frequently help the owners with this task.

Black Down
Haslemere

1.6km (1 mile) southeast of Haslemere. Car parking off Tennyson's lane on the northern edge of the property. (SU920308) 303 ha (749 acres) AONB
National Trust

You can see Black Down from miles around. At 280 metres – the highest point in West Sussex – the wood is a dominant feature of the local landscape.

With astonishing views, almost year-round colour and a wide variety of woodland birds it is not surprising this has been regarded as a beauty spot since Victorian times.

The wettest place in the Weald, this National Trust site offers common, heathland, ancient and more recent woodland.

Quellwood Common is a diverse ancient broadleaved woodland on Black Down's southern slopes where two rock types meet to produce a hummocky landscape scored with springs and streams. The steep, sandy eastern side supports mature beech woods.

Much of the once extensive heathland has been colonised. Pine woods cloak the steep slopes of Black Down where glades add interest. The best areas of heath - at their colourful best in summer - are on the down's south west flank.

MAP 2

Ebernoe Common Nature Reserve
Northchapel

Take the A283 north from
Petworth. After about 5km
(3 miles), take the minor road right
(first road outside the town).
Follow this winding road until you
reach a red phone box. About
10m further on the right the
entrance is marked 'Ebernoe
Church'. (SU976278)
72 ha (178 acres) SSSI
Sussex Wildlife Trust

Historically and ecologically
fascinating, Ebernoe Common
Nature Reserve is an
outstanding example of low
Weald woodland.

Remote, teeming with
wildlife, the site has wood
pasture, ponds, streams and
flower-rich meadow while
surrounding farmland is being
converted back to woodland.

Lichens – rare outside the
New Forest – thrive here, as do
13 species of British bat,
dormice and a host of birds.

The oak and ash-dominated
site – hit by the storms of 1987
– now features a wide age-
range of trees including some
beautiful, gnarled ancient
specimens. The rides and glades
support many floral species.

Remnants of a small
brickworks can be seen on the
common, including the brick
kiln, now a scheduled ancient
monument.

Visitors are advised to go
prepared with sturdy boots and
a plan – while flat it is often
wet underfoot and the plethora
of paths can make it difficult to
find your way.

MAP 2

Mens Nature Reserve
Petworth

Take the A272 east from Petworth. After about 6.5km (4 miles), turn right at crossroads in the middle of a large wood, signposted Hawkhurst Court. Car park 100m on right. (TQ023237)
159 ha (393 acres)
AONB SSSI

Sussex Wildlife Trust

The Mens Nature Reserve is something of an ancient wilderness where Nature has been allowed to reign unchallenged for more than a century.

Once used for timber production, woodland management of the site was abandoned about 120 years ago, leaving it to grow untamed.

There is much to discover here by following a waymarked trail from the car park but wear sturdy boots since the paths are often narrow and muddy – even in summer.

Huge, towering beech stand out in a forest with trees of all

Mens Nature Reserve

sizes and ages. Notable among the oaks is the vast Idehurst Oak with a girth of more than six metres.

Open areas are few but Badlands Meadow in the southeast has an impressive display of summer flowers including lady's mantle and dyers greenwood.

The site sustains a wealth of birds – nuthatch, blackcap, woodpecker as well as butterflies such as the purple emperor, white admiral and silver-washed fritillary.

Binton & Britty Woods
Farnham

South of the A31 and west of the A3. Head south from Seale towards Elstead. Car parking is on the right just before crossroads with Littleworth Road, after about 800m (0.5 mile). (SU895465)
100 ha (247 acres) AONB
Hampton Estate

Spring is a good time to visit the Hampton Estate when bluebells add a splash of colour to the woodland landscape of Binton and Britty woods.

A circular walk connects both of the woods, which are commercially managed for timber production, with wooded Puttenham Common and the North Downs Way.

The bluebells grow in Binton, a 41-hectare site with a clear 'north–south' division – the northern side dominated by sweet chestnut coppice while the southern is given over to pine, fir and larch.

A waymarked trail on the easy, sandy soils of Binton can be completed in about an hour, providing plenty of opportunity to move on to neighbouring Britty Wood.

Occasional oaks and Corsican pines dot the landscape of this 62-hectare site, which is dominated by Scots pine. A single main route weaves through its central shallow valley with occasional woodland paths providing additional opportunities to explore its gentle to moderate slopes.

MAP 2

Witley Common
Witley

11km (7 miles) southwest of Guildford between the A3 and the A286. 1.6km (1 mile) southwest of Milford. Signposted from A3. (SU933407)

152 ha (376 acres) AONB SSSI

National Trust

Visitors – particularly children – can get fun out of their 'hands-on' experience of nature, while the grown-ups enjoy a leisurely stroll around Witley Common.

This National Trust site, a combination of heathland, woodland, scrub, grassland and ponds, has good recreation, education and interactive facilities, including a children's nature trail.

Easy walking along well-maintained waymarked trails provides access to the heathland of Witley Common where three types of heather create eye-catching late summer colour, and mixed woodland that has evolved over 60 years on land formerly used for grazing.

Impressive tall stands of Scots pine and large, imposing sweet chestnuts alternate with grassy areas and glades, one of which was used as a parade ground by troops during both world wars.

The woods support three species of woodpecker. The wheelchair-accessible visitor centre, which hosts excellent children's events, provides further information.

Durfold Wood
Dunsfold

From Chiddingfold village green head southeast on Pickhurst Road which becomes Fisher Lane. About half a mile before a right-hand bend and 100m before the Plaistow Road T-junction, turn sharp right into small car park. (SU987326)
18 ha (44 acres) AONB
Woodland Trust

War games were once played among the oak trees of Durfold Wood but today it is a peaceful part of the Surrey countryside.

Set well away from main roads, it is a light and airy site within the much larger Chiddingfold Forest Site of Special Scientific Interest.

Man has made numerous changes to this semi-natural ancient woodland over the years, practically clearing it during both world wars. Therefore few very old trees remain.

Dormice, butterflies and moths, reptiles, insects and birds thrive here, among them woodcock, tawny owl, lesser-spotted woodpecker and even nightingales.

Work to improve habitats includes tree thinning, ride-widening and traditional hedge-laying. The public bridleway across the southern end connects with the Sussex Border Path.

Durfold Wood

MAP 2

Winterfold Forest
Albury

From the A254 Guildford to
Dorking road, take the A248
(signposted Godalming). After
800m (0.5 mile) cross small bridge,
then turn left into New Road up
hill over level crossing to Farley
Green, then left at village green
into Shophouse Lane, then 1.6km
(1 mile) to forest sign.
(TQ065435) 135 ha (334 acres)
AONB
Mr J A McAllister

No matter how many times
you return to Winterfold
Forest, part of the extensive
Hurt Wood area of the North
Downs, there is always more
to explore.

Mainly privately owned, it
has been open to the public for
almost 80 years. 30 miles of
public rights of way run
through the site plus another
30 miles of unofficial tracks
and a choice of 12 car parks

Hurt Wood – named after the
bilberry or 'hurts' that grow
here – covers more than 1,200
hectares of heath and
woodland on the greensand
ridge. From the southern
escarpment ridge, among fine
tall beech trees, are panoramic
views across the Weald.

The slope is broken by valleys
and streams where oak, birch,
rowan and sweet chestnut
abound. Elsewhere, tall Scots
pine dominate, with bracken
and bilberry providing autumn
colour at their feet.

Fir Tree Copse
Godalming/Haslemere

Southeast of Dunsfold on road to
Alford Crossways and Horsham,
take second right turn after 3km
(2 miles) into Rams Lane. Follow
car park signs to Forestry
Commission site at Sidney Wood.
(TQ023350) 6 ha (14 acres) SSSI
Surrey Wildlife Trust

Perfect for a peaceful interlude,
Fir Tree Copse is a quiet
woodland in the heart of a
much larger wooded habitat.

Beautiful, tall straight oak and
ash trees dominate the site
with hazel coppice beneath.
Light and shade is created
thanks to a programme of re-
coppicing, which has formed
glades, allowing light back onto
the woodland floor.

A distinctive, small clump of Scots pine that stands in its southwestern section probably gives the wood its name.

Colour comes from a host of woodland flowers including bluebell, wood anemone, dog's mercury, enchanter's nightshade, pignut, lily-of-the-valley and wild daffodil. Further interest is provided by marshland species that grow on the northwest boundary, site of the now derelict Wey and Arun canal.

Routes through the site are well waymarked on passable, if narrow paths. A round tour takes just 30 minutes, leaving ample time to explore surrounding woodland.

Cucknells Wood
Godalming

Turn off B2128 about 1.6km (1 mile) south-east of Shamley Green into Stroud Lane. Wood is on left after approx. 500m (0.3 mile). (TQ041430)
10 ha (25 acres)

Surrey Wildlife Trust

Bluebell, foxglove, primrose, common-spotted orchid, yellow pimpernel, bugle – just some of the many colourful flowers on show in this peaceful wood.

Narrow paths wind around large oaks, ash, birch and rowan, coppiced hazel, holly hawthorn, wild cherry and crab apple. In the centre of the wood is a surprise group of Norway spruce, planted as Christmas trees.

Northwards the landscape becomes wetter with a carpet of soft mosses growing beneath alders. Snake's Alley, a damp open space in the northwest, supports a good range of insect life.

In spring migrant birds, including chiffchaff, willow warbler and blackcap, join the resident population of nuthatch, marsh and willow tits, tawny owl, tree-creeper and three woodpecker species.

A waymarked walk offers a pleasant half hour stroll. The route is well signed leading along narrow paths and across sleeper bridges over the stream.

Nearby Winterfold (see previous page) provides a wonderful contrast in scale and character.

MAP 2

Sheepleas
Between West and East Horsley

From Leatherhead take the A246
to East Horsley. In East Horsley
turn south into Chalk Lane and
then right into Greendene where
the car park can be found on the
right. Alternatively, continue on the
A246 through East Horsley and
park in the car park in Epsom
Road adjacent to St Mary's
Church. (TQ080514)
108 ha (267 acres) AONB SSSI
Surrey Wildlife Trust

One could easily get lost in the
maze of permissive paths and
rights of way that weave
through this section of the
North Downs.

There is a great variety of
habitats including mature beech
and oak woodland, plantations,
hazel coppice, scrub and

meadow with two waymarked
trails (if occasionally confusing)
and a self-guided circular trail.

Close to the car park is a
picnic area and, not far from
here, a Millennium viewpoint
offering views extending to
Canary Wharf, the Post Office
Tower and other London
landmarks.

Renowned for its chalkland
flora, the site supports quaking
grass, rock rose, eyebright,
milkwort, common-spotted and
fragrant orchids. In the mixed
woodland you'll find coppiced
sections, yew and box walks,
some magnificent beeches and
attractive glades animated with
butterflies by day and bats
at night.

Common blue, green
hairstreak, grizzled skipper and
silver-washed fritillary are
among the 30 species of
butterfly recorded here.

Ranmore
Dorking

3km (2 miles) north-west of
Dorking on unclassified road to
East Horsley. Adjacent to southern
boundary of Polesden Lacey Estate
which is approached on the A246
2.5km (1.5 miles) from Bookham.
(TQ142504) 266 ha (657 acres)

AONB SSSI
National Trust

Beautiful. That is the word that
sums up Ranmore, a huge
ancient wooded common on
the North Downs

This is a local landmark, providing delightful views from the Ranmore Common road and from the gardens at Polesden Lacey.

Just as delightful to discover from within, it features huge mature beech, oak and yew trees adorning the slopes of the downs, divided by gently sloping wooded valleys.

There is something to enjoy all year round in this cool, quiet and peaceful site where a variety of paths provide a network through wide and open areas and beneath the closed canopy of trees. The going can get wet and muddy, so sturdy footwear is recommended.

Even though access doesn't appear to be actively promoted, this is a woodland to be enjoyed by all. Visitors without transport of their own can use the local explorer bus or walk from Polesden Lacey through Ranmore.

Nearby is the Woodland Trust's 70-acre Great Ridings Wood (TQ105539).

Ranmore

MAP 2

Leith Hill
Coldharbour, Dorking
Northwest of the A29; west of the
A24; south of the A25.
(TQ132428) 270 ha (667 acres)
AONB SSSI
National Trust

Close to the conifer
plantations of Abinger and
Wotton Commons is tower-
topped Leith Hill from where,
on a clear day, you can see
across 13 counties.

The hill is served by lots of
paths and tracks – many of
them steep and rough. Athletic
visitors can tackle the strenuous
climb through the woods to the
base of the Leith Hill tower.

During spring and summer
the southern slopes are ablaze
with colour from a
rhododendron wood planted in

Leith Hill

1900 by Charles Darwin's sister, Caroline Wedgwood.

Beech and pine grow in steep gulleys on the scarp face but the main woodland – birch, oak and beech – lies on the greensand ridge. Particularly stunning is Severells Copse with beautiful oak over birch coppice.

The arboretum either side of the Coldharbour has some impressive redwoods and exotic species to marvel at.

Nightjars, adders and lizards are making their homes in new glades being created by the National Trust.

Leechpool & Owlbeech Woods

Horsham

To the east of Horsham town centre just off the B2195 (Harwood Road). (TQ194314) 34 ha (84 acres)

Horsham District Council

Popular, well cared for and full of variety, Leechpool and Owlbeech Woods are a great place for children and adults alike.

Roe deer can be spotted in both these contrasting woods, which are served by two waymarked routes.

Leechpool is a mixed woodland site of oak, beech, sweet chestnut, Scots pine and holly where a good variety of spring flowering plants add interest and a whole range of birds – including chiffchaff and nuthatch – thrives.

Contrasting Owlbeech is made up of conifers and heathland, with cool alders, ferns and mosses. It supports a number of birds and visiting fallow deer. Fungi add interest in the autumn and a stream running through the wood sustains amphibians and dragonflies.

The site is well served by formal and informal paths - occasionally muddy - and well-maintained boardwalks over the wet areas of the alder woodland.

The High Weald Landscape Trail crosses St Leonard's Forest (almost adjoining), a large Forestry Commission plantation including Scots and Corsican pine.

MAP 2

Nymans
Handcross

On the B2114 at Handcross, just off the London to Brighton (M23/A23) road. (TQ265297) 100 ha (247 acres) AONB SSSI

National Trust

There are a host of features to enjoy on any of a number of enjoyable walks through the exceptional woodland of the Nymans estate.

The woods, which occupy 100 hectares of the 243-hectare estate, lie in the valley and are accessible only via steep slopes and steps.

Used at various times to serve the iron, leather-tanning and boat-building industries, the woods today are peaceful and well maintained. They are managed for public access and wildlife, which thrives among the gnarled old beeches and oaks of the steep-sided ghylls.

Close to a delightful avenue of tall conifers can be found Sussex's third tallest tree – a Wellingtonia – which lost its 'tallest tree' title after lightning destroyed its top in the 1990s.

Three waymarked routes through ancient woodland and conifer plantations follow a route beside a large central lake and past various archaeological features and are extended in spring to include a bluebell walk through Pookchurch wood.

Nymans Wood

Hammond's Copse
Newdigate

From A24/A25 roundabout in Dorking take A24 south and left into Chart Lane. After 1.6km (1 mile) turn left into Red Lane. At next T-junction turn right and right again at next T-junction and right into Broad Lane. Copse on your left, two entrances, better parking at southern entrance next to derelict chapel. (TQ212441)
30 ha (74 acres)
Woodland Trust

An opportunity to find out how good management can return ancient woodland sites such as this to their former glory.

There are more than 3.5 miles of well-maintained paths ranging from open sunny rides to mysterious narrow routes deep in the heart of the wood, and a waymarked nature trail.

A large pond with a marshy area at the centre of the wood is home to dragonflies and newts. On your walk listen for tawny owls, watch sparrowhawks in flight and catch a glimpse of colourful butterflies such as silver-washed fritillary, yellow brimstone and white admiral.

In spring migrant chiffchaffs and blackcaps sing above colourful splashes of bluebell and wild daffodil. Look also for guelder rose, wild service tree, wood and wood spurge – all species typical of ancient woodland. An information leaflet is available to guide visitors.

There are three other Woodland Trust sites nearby that you may also like to visit: Glover's Wood (TQ227406), Edolph's Wood (TQ236424) and Rickett's Wood (TQ230428).

MAP 2

Box Hill

Dorking

From the A24, turn east on to B2209 at Westhumble. Turn east after
400m (0.25m) – signed to Box Hill. (TQ180513)
217 ha (536 acres) AONB SSSI

National Trust

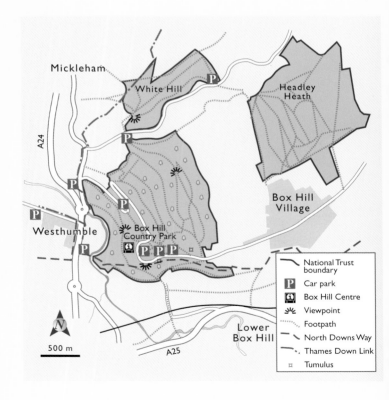

More than a million visitors a year flock to Box Hill, a beautiful blend of downland and woodland that dominates the countryside north of Dorking.

Dotted with many interesting features, this is an historic site. As well as two Bronze Age burial mounds, the Roman road of Stane Street linking Chichester with London crosses the site. Remains of a Romano-British settlement have been discovered nearby.

Box Hill fort, constructed in 1899, was built to help protect London from the threat of invasion. Today it is colonised by several species of bat. John Logie Baird conducted his TV experiments at the summit.

Dramatic scarp slopes, known as the Whites, rise up from the River Mole where stepping stones indicate an ancient crossing point.

Teeming with birds, bats and butterflies as well as people, it features no fewer than 400 species of flowering plant and 58 species of butterfly. Generations of visitors have enjoyed the stunning views from its busy summit – one of the highest points on the North Downs.

Woodland covers more than half the site. Named after the renowned box trees that grow on its steep chalk slopes, the plateau area also supports oak and ash with wild cherry, birch and rowan. There are beautiful large beech trees and some magnificent yews, some estimated to be over 250 years old.

Designated a Country Park in 1971, facilities today are good with an information centre, shop, picnic area, café and a choice of car parks. Children will enjoy the family fun trail and summer events.

At particularly busy times it is probably best to avoid the summit and explore further afield. There are many alternatives to choose from including a number of waymarked routes ranging from 1–5 hours. Leaflets describing each route, including a two-hour nature trail, are available from the shop.

MAP 2

Norbury Park
Leatherhead

From the A24 south of
Leatherhead turn west at the
roundabout onto the A246
towards Fetcham. Young Street car
park is on the left just before the
railway bridge. Or continue on
A246 and take first left on
roundabout at top of hill for
Fetcham and Bocketts Farm car
parks. (TQ158538)
526 ha (1300 acres) AONB, SSSI
Surrey County Council

Recreation, relaxation and
education are all well catered
for at Norbury Park.

This popular site combines
multi-purpose woodland,
farmland and chalk grassland
offering wonderful views and
excellent access. The various
features to be found here
include a three-hour woodland
management demonstration
trail illustrating how the site is
being used for timber
production, wildlife
conservation and visitors alike.

The woodland and chalk
grassland area is a designated
SSSI featuring yew, ash, cherry,
oak, hazel and sweet chestnut
coppice and an ancient yew
section known as Druids
Grove. Some areas were hit by
the storms of 1987, which
opened the way for new
plantations.

Public and permissive routes,
a self-guided circular trail, a
permanent orienteering course
and family off-road cycle route
all help to keep the most active
visitor busy. Thought to be one
of the Mickleham manors
mentioned in the *Domesday
Book*, Norbury was purchased
by Surrey County Council to
shield it from development.

Ashtead Common
Ashtead

Approaching Ashtead from the A24, turn down Woodfield Lane opposite the Leg of Mutton and Cauliflower pub. Continue down the lane for 800m (0.5mile), straight over two mini roundabouts towards railway station. Over level crossing, turn left, park on the side of road, Common lies in front of you. (TQ180590)
210 ha (500 acres) SSSI
Corporation of London

Ashtead Common is a fabulous mosaic of grassland, wetland, scrub and woodland, boasting magnificent old trees.

Set on a ridge, with good views across the surrounding landscape, Ashtead was declared a National Nature Reserve in 1995. Good paths – some suitable for wheelchairs – lead through a succession of habitats.

For centuries, around 2,000 ancient oaks – some up to 400 years old – have been cropped to manage the wood. Little grows on the woodland floor but the great old boughs of many of these mature fungi-clad 'pollards' are riddled with nooks and crannies providing homes for bats, owls, woodpeckers, treecreepers and nuthatches. This deadwood sustains 1,000 species of beetle, 150 of them rare.

Look out too for grass snakes, adders, lizards and purple emperor butterflies. The southern marsh orchid also grows here.

While in the area, Ashtead Park is also worth a visit with its veteran trees, woodland, meadows and ponds.

Beetles thrive at Ashtead

MAP 2

Banstead Woods
Chipstead/Banstead

Follow the B2219 (Holly Lane)
from Banstead for 3km (2 miles).
Large car park on right.
Chipstead Station 300m.
(TQ273593)
115 ha (284 acres) SSSI
**Reigate and Banstead
Borough Council**

Popular with walkers, joggers,
children and dog owners,
beautiful Banstead is a joy to
discover – though the hour or
so it takes to cover the site
throws up some challenging
inclines.

There is a grand feeling to
this large ancient woodland set
on the edge of a steep slope. It
boasts commanding views of
the local landscape – and a
sense of the past.

The site features some big old
oaks and beech trees along
with sweet chestnuts, silver
birch, wild cherries and
coppiced hazel. At the top of
the wood there is a small
woodland pond.

Despite the numbered
waymarker posts, you can get
lost in Banstead but thanks to
the grid-like system of paths
you're soon back on track.
Most of the paths are wide and
compacted, lending a sense of
space and grandness to the
wood.

Cycling and horse riding are
not permitted.

Wimbledon & Putney Commons
Wimbledon

Take Windmill Road, off Parkside
(A219). Road leads to golf
clubhouse and the windmill.
(TQ221720)
456 ha (1127 acres) SSSI
**The Board of Wimbledon &
Putney Commons Conservators**

Wimbledon and neighbouring
Putney commons have all you
could ask for an enjoyable day
'wandering free'.

Here you will discover areas
of oak and birch, beech and
hornbeam woodland, heathland
with large lakes, man-made
ponds and acidic spring bogs –
a range of landscapes for
visitors on foot, horseback and
cycle to explore.

The extensive mature

woodland and open space makes it easy to forget you are just a stone's throw from Central London and you feel as though you are in the countryside. Low-flying golf balls can let you know that courses are nearby.

While there is a good network of well-surfaced paths, it is possible to lose your way. The woodland is a wonderful area with big and beautiful oak and beech contrasting with areas of dense undergrowth. This is a great place to enjoy bluebells in spring.

The open grassland is good for ground nesting birds during late spring and early summer.

Kew Gardens
Richmond

Enter by Brentford Gate via Kew Green and Ferry Lane. Other entrances – Main Gate (off Kew Green), Victoria Gate (off Kew Road) and Lion Gate (off Kew Road). (TQ189768)
49 ha (121 acres)
Royal Botanic Gardens Kew

Very different and much more formal than other sites featured in this guide, Kew will be of considerable interest to anyone who enjoys woodland and trees.

As well as visiting the glasshouses and flower gardens, a couple of hours spent in the more wooded western part of the grounds will be a rewarding experience. This area has a parkland feel with many native and exotic trees growing over mown grass.

A riverside walk with good views over the Thames leads through birch, chestnuts and poplars and past some fine oaks. In the northwestern corner is a conservation area managed as native woodland and famed for its carpet of bluebells each May.

A stroll through the grounds brings constant surprises -- around the next corner could be an imposing giant redwood or an unusually elegant conifer. A 'deadwood felled area' has been created as a landscape feature and a habitat for wildlife, particularly stag beetles.

MAP 2

Joydens Wood
Bexley South
Southeast London, west of A2018 south of Old Bexley. (TQ501717)
135 ha (333 acres)
Woodland Trust

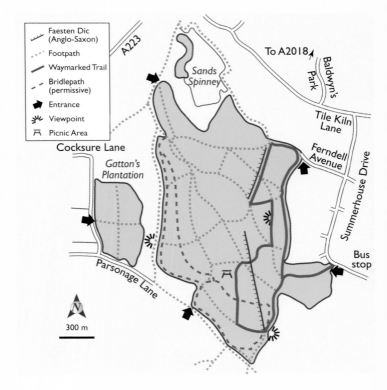

Set on a hilltop just 21km (13 miles) from the heart of London, is Joydens Wood.

Look carefully and you will see relics of its history including banks, ditches, humps and hollows beneath the trees, the remains of two late Iron Age roundhouses which are more than 2000 years old and the Faesten Dic, an Anglo-Saxon defensive bank and ditch running through the wood.

In the centre a series of banks or lynchets provides evidence that the area was farmed in the Middle Ages. Small depressions in the ground indicate deneholes where underlying chalk was mined to spread on fields in an effort to try and improve the poor soil. Not being very productive land it was abandoned and trees reclaimed the soil.

A leaflet produced jointly by the Woodland Trust and the Archaeological Unit of Cambridgeshire County Council explains how, for thousands of years, people have been altering Joydens Wood to suit their different purposes.

This hilly site is popular with local walkers and is open for cycling on main tracks. It also

Joydens Wood

has a permit riding scheme.

Despite being replanted with Corsican pine in the 1950s, the site has a wide variety of native trees, shrubs and flowers, which the owners are working to increase. Coppicing and clearing of the rides is helping to create a more open character to the wood.

As more light enters, increased flowers, butterflies, birds and insects appear. Wood ants are one of many minibeasts that respond well to the increased sunlight, to the delight of green woodpeckers, which catch them on their long sticky tongues. A colourful collection of fungi can also be found.

Chalk Wood, to the south, is ancient woodland dominated by oak, silver birch and sweet chestnut and is well worth a visit.

MAP 2

Sheen Common
Richmond

From A205 Richmond Road, take
B351 Sheen Lane. Turn right onto
Christchurch Road and at mini
roundabout go straight on to Fife
Road. Park on roadside as road
bends to left. Keep playing fields on
left and enter wood. (TQ197745)
21 ha (52 acres)
London Borough of Richmond

Just a stone's throw from the
delights of Richmond Park lies
the dense woodland of Sheen
Common, a haven for wildlife

Though rich in trees, there
are still patches of grassland
with wild heather in open
glades, lending it a spacious
feel. The area is a favourite
haunt of dog owners and a
popular gateway into the park,
with a good network of paths.

The area was an open
common used for grazing until
the 1930s but, since then, has
become rich in rowan, holly
and sycamore, and has some
beautifully shaped oaks with
open crowns and a 150-year-
old plane tree – one of the
common's oldest.

Observant visitors might spot
foxes, woodpeckers, speckled
wood butterflies and even
badgers. The pond in the
northern section of the site is
good for frogs, toads and
beetles, despite the sometimes
orange hue of the water caused
by iron deposits in the soil.

Lesnes Abbey Wood
Belvedere

Abbey Road (B213) is to east of
A2041 in Belvedere. (TQ478787)
88 ha (217 acres) SSSI
Bexley Council

Lesnes Abbey is a treasure
trove of natural and
archaeological discoveries
where you can forget the
bustle of the nearby capital.

The broadleaved woodland
around the abbey ruins
includes impressive hornbeam
and unusual exotics. It comes
alive in warmer months with
bluebells and wild daffodils in
spring and colourful St John's
wort, willow herbs and yellow
archangel in the summer.

Woodpeckers, kestrels and
tawny owls share the woods,
unusually, with ring-necked

parakeets. Yellow iris, reedmace, frogs and the occasional grey heron can be spotted around the ponds.

Self-guided trails around the site offer good views across the Thames towards London and include interesting features such as 'Sleeping Dryad' – a

sweet chestnut with a face.

Venture into open heathland in the heart of the wood and look for butterflies, insects and birds. The mounds here are thought to be the remains of an ancient burial site. In some sections fossils have been uncovered.

Sydenham Hill Wood
Upper Sydenham

The main entrance is in Crescent Wood Road, SE26, off Sydenham Hill. (TQ344724)
10 ha (25 acres)
London Wildlife Trust

Those with an interest in wildlife or history will reap rewards on a visit to Sydenham Hill Wood – a site with plenty of variety and interest.

Part of the Great North Wood, an ancient woodland straddling the ridge between Deptford, Streatham and Selhurst, it is a great place for butterflies in the summer.

Quite dense in places, there are contrasting, more-open clearings where trees – oaks, hornbeam, sycamore and ash among them – have fallen in storms.

Numbered posts – not the easiest to follow – take visitors on a figure-of-eight tour of the wood, part of which was once incorporated into the gardens of Victorian villas. Little remains of these old houses today but you might discover the remains of an old tennis court and Victorian folly.

Dead wood, left for the benefit of wildlife, provides nesting places for the lesser spotted woodpeckers – look out too for bullfinches and hawkfinches.

MAP 2

Petts Wood & Hawkwood
Chislehurst

Park in Chislehurst and walk southeast along the main road A208. The woods lie to the southwest of the road. (TQ450687) 134 ha (331 acres)
National Trust

Petts Wood and Hawkwood is a surprisingly peaceful woodland where the sound of birdsong helps you escape the noise of nearby road and rail traffic and into a natural world of tranquility.

Careful management (explained in warm tones by the warden's note at the entrance to the site) and natural regeneration contribute to the interest of this site. There is a variety of tree species including some big old pollarded oaks, young emerging trees and lovely, big, twisted specimens in which children can explore and hide.

Clearings have been maintained as part of a heathland creation project where dead standing trees provide wonderful nesting posts and insect habitats.

The west of the wood overlooks Tongs Farm, an open meadow where sheep graze and which produces a wonderful show of wildflowers in spring/summer.

The wood is surrounded by Chiselhurst and St Paul's Cray commons with Scadbury Nature Reserve just over the road.

Bramley Bank
Croydon

Main entrance at bottom of Riesco Drive, off Ballards Way, South Croydon. Limited car parking in Riesco Drive or in large District Council car park on left of Riesco Drive. (TQ352634) 11 ha (27 acres)
London Wildlife Trust

Delightful views, clear paths, ponds, varied woodland and a busy wildlife population all contribute to make Bramley Bank an enjoyable place to explore.

This is a well-walked wood with a circular route allowing visitors to enjoy a host of interesting features including great views over nearby fields to more distant, urban landscapes.

The London Loop follows the eastern side of the wood and is waymarked. Clear and well-trodden paths lead by large oaks and at least one majestic-looking beech to a large pond in its northern section. A little murky and shaded, it is lined with lilies and supports a number of moorhens and other wildlife, which comes here to drink.

Elsewhere, look for standing deadwood trunks which display markings of woodpeckers and burrowing insects.

Mature secondary woodland populated with sycamore, sweet chestnut, ash, and silver birch stand above bramble, bracken and young regenerating trees.

Shoreham Woods
Shoreham

11km (7 miles) north of Sevenoaks off A224. Junction 4 off M25, take the A224 to Dunton Green. At next roundabout take first exit, Shacklands Road to Shoreham. Car park 250m on right. (TQ501616) 101 ha (250 acres) AONB
Sevenoaks District Council

It is easy to immerse yourself in this collection of woods, despite a nearby motorway.

A network of footpaths enable you to explore the woods of Jenkins Neck, Barnetts, Meenfield, Pilots, and Andrew's Wood, an ancient woodland site with displays of yellow archangel, dog's mercury, bluebell and foxglove.

Conifer plantations are being thinned and replanted with broadleaves. Look out for a magnificent beech tree surrounded by younger trees and a beautifully carved seat on the eastern side of Andrew's Wood.

Across the motorway, areas of oak supporting dense vegetation beneath contrast strikingly with the neighbouring beech with its sparse understorey.

To the east of Meenfield Wood, wonderful views extend over the Darent Valley toward Shoreham village. Look for a memorial cross cut into the hillside.

The varied bird population includes treecreeper, chaffinch and kestrel. Look out for purple hairstreak or white admiral butterflies and, on a sunny day, you may spot a common lizard warming itself.

MAP 2

Marden Park
Woldingham

Follow Northdown Road, south of
Woldingham and right into
Gangers Hill. Car park on right
after S-bend. If coming from M25,
take junction 6 and A22 south. At
roundabout turn left onto A25.
After 800m turn left into Tandridge
Hill Lane. At T-junction right into

Gangers Hill, car park on left.
(TQ369539) 63 ha (156 acres)
Woodland Trust

High on the South Downs,
within the Surrey Hills Area of
Outstanding Natural Beauty,
you will find Marden Park
Woods, the largest Woodland
Trust site in the county.

Marden Park

This expanse of varying woodland habitats – a bit of a draw for visitors – is actually made up of Marden Park and Great Church Wood.

This is an area of great diversity from ancient woodland to large expanses of developing woods and stretches of recreated chalk grassland where plants such as common, bee and greater butterfly orchids thrive.

As a result this is a rich haven of wildlife with no fewer than 25 species of butterfly, rare snails and stripe-winged grasshoppers.

The North Downs Way and the six-mile Woldingham Countryside Walk both run through the site, which is well served by an extensive network of maintained permissive footpaths, while a surfaced bridleway allows riders a safe route through part of the woods.

Graeme Hendrey Wood
Bletchingley

Take Rabies Heath Road east from Bletchingley. Park in Tilburstow Hill car park on right. (TQ346501)
10 ha (25 acres)
Surrey Wildlife Trust

Graeme Hendrey Wood is an unusual mixed woodland that has grown up in an old sand quarry on the lower greensand ridge.

Even if you don't have the stamina required to tackle some of its challenging inclines, you can enjoy the view from the car park – with wonderful vistas across the Weald.

Quarrying seems to have been carried out in long, deep ridges – hence the unusual and uneven landscape. The humid and wet conditions in the old hollows provide a perfect habitat for liverworts, mosses and ferns.

Some of the inclines are extremely steep but local volunteers have come up with a clever solution – creating steps and paths out of tree trunks.

Lots of young trees are emerging among the birch, ash, oak, beech, sweet chestnut and ample sycamore. Woodland flowers abound too – look out for bitter vetch, broadleaved helleborine orchid, townhall clock, wood speedwell and yellow pimpernel.

MAP 2

Great & Little Earls Woods
Oxted

In Limpsfield take Wolf's Row south, off A25. Road becomes Pollards Wood and then Reed Lane. Just after Merle Common Road joins from right, woodland appears on right. Near Royal Oak pub on left is parking and entrance with an information board. (TQ406489) 10 ha (25 acres)
Woodland Trust

The ancient woodlands of Great & Little Earls Woods form the western extremity of a much larger expanse of woodland in this area. Most is designated a Site of Special Scientific Interest.

Sweet chestnut is still coppiced in the south of Great Earls Wood but this gives way to a high forest of oak and sweet chestnut in the north. Little Earls Wood to the northwest has a delightful area of old hornbeam coppice.

Great & Little Earls are locally known for their fantastic display of bluebells in spring. Bracken, honeysuckle and creeping soft grass are also abundant and grow alongside a number of ancient woodland indicator species.

A small pond is located in the centre of a recently created conservation ride and this is fed by a seasonal stream which runs the length of the ride.

Visitors benefit from a good network of well-maintained paths and three information boards.

Toys Hill
Westerham

4km (2.5 miles) south of Brasted, 1.6km (1 mile) west of Ide Hill. Car park close to the Fox & Hounds public house. (TQ465517) 194 ha (479 acres) SSSI
National Trust

The storms that lashed Britain in 1987 changed the face of Toys Hill and their legacy is evident today.

Designated a location of national importance for nature conservation, it is part of a band of hilltop woods and sustains a good selection of woodland plants, birds and

Toys Hill

mammals. Rich in insects and fauna, it also produces an excellent selection of fungi in the autumn.

Much of the site's storm-damaged timber was cleared but around a quarter was left to rot, to encourage wildlife. The worst-hit sections – on the plateau – are now regenerating vigorously while lower down, mature oak, birch and pine grow in a sheltered and tranquil vale.

In contrast, the north- and east-facing slopes of the site – at 235 metres Kent's highest point – suffered little damage and here you can enjoy the full beauty of Toys Hill as it was pre-1987. Longer routes through the site lead to beautiful mature woodland.

MAP 2

Stubbs Wood (Hanging Bank)
Ide Hill

800m (0.5 mile) east of the Ide Hill along the B2042, turn right on to minor road at Y-junction. Parking 450m on right. (TQ498518)
40 ha (99 acres)
Kent County Council

Stubbs Wood, also known as Hanging Bank, lies on the scarp face of the greensand ridge in Kent, overlooking the Weald.

Indeed, the Greensand Way – a long-distance footpath between Haslemere in Surrey and Hamstreet near Ashford in Kent – crosses the site.

The occasional Scots pine interrupts a site where sweet chestnut dominates a broadleaf coppice mix that also includes beech, oak and rowan. Butterflies, including the speckled wood and white admiral, are also to be found.

Visitors keen to tackle the circular walk within the wood should be prepared for some steep climbs, since it undulates along the scarp slope and can be slippery, particularly in winter or after it has rained.

Persevere and be rewarded with occasional views out over the Weald and in particular, some lovely views from Ide Hill to the west.

Look out for birdboxes along the main path at the top of the ridge.

Speckled Wood butterfly

Staffhurst Wood
Oxted

From A25 south through
Limpsfield Common to Grants
Lane (TQ471 4485)
38 ha (94 acres) SSSI
**Surrey Wildlife Trust/
Woodland Trust**

Part of a large woodland block
designated of Special Scientific
Interest, Staffhurst is a
nationally important ancient
wooded common, rich in
species.

It also has in interesting
history – and dates back at least
to Saxon times when it was
part of a royal hunting forest.
During the Second World War
the woodland was used as an
ammunitions dump.

Dominated by oak and beech
high forest, the mosaic of semi
natural stands of mixed age and
species includes a sparse
understorey of scattered birch,
hornbeam, yew and holly. The
area is covered by a tree
preservation order.

The site has more than 200
species of flora, including the
thin-spiked wood sedge, which
is rare in Surrey, and 288 species
of moth – in fact this is the
best-known English location for
one, orthosis populeti.

Largely level, the wood is
dissected by a number of paths,
including four public footpaths,
but there are no public
bridleways.

Frosted holly

MAP 2

Ashdown Forest
Uckfield, Crowborough, East Grinstead

A22 to Wych Cross crossroads, turn east for 1.6km (1 mile) to Forest Centre (TQ433324)

2467 ha (6097 acres) AONB SSSI

Ashdown Forest Trust

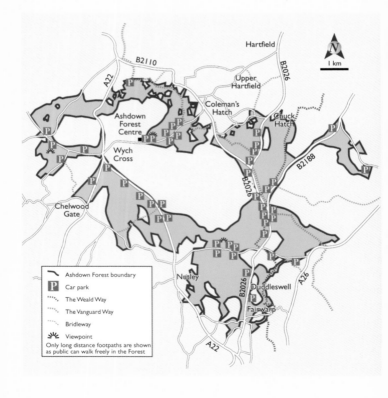

Ashdown Forest

Centuries of change, natural and man-made, have helped to shape the 10 square miles of heathland and woodland that make up Ashdown Forest, a site drawing more than a million people annually.

Visitors are well catered for with 50 car parks, extensive rides and footpaths, activities such as horse riding (with a permit), kite flying – even golf – and a Forest Centre. Yet a short walk is all it takes to transport the visitor to quieter areas of beauty.

Wildlife thrives at Ashdown, with a sizeable bird population including nightjar and woodcock, no fewer than 34 different butterfly species and

MAP 2

around half Britain's 46 breeding species of damselflies and dragonflies.

Heathland – the largest expanse in the southeast and nearly 5 per cent of all that remains in Britain – is the star attraction here. Stunningly beautiful, it supports some of the country's rarest wildlife and an abundance of colourful heathers.

A forest in the oldest sense of the word, Ashdown was created for deer hunting and today supports four different species.

Woodland, which makes up around 40 per cent of the site, is extensive. While most woods on the site were cleared at some time to make charcoal for the iron industry, a handful are believed to be ancient. Today there is a wide variety of trees: pendunculate oak and silver birch are interspersed with beech, birch and sycamore, sweet chestnut, field maple, ash and hazel and clumps of Scots pine, planted in the 19th century.

Older sections are richest in flora while damper sections of the woods have an abundance of ferns including the rare marsh fern, found on just a few other sites in Sussex.

A. A. Milne used the Forest's wonderful settings as inspiration for the many adventures of Winnie the Pooh.

Pooh Sticks bridge

Lake Wood

Lake Wood
Uckfield

Follow Church Street west out of Uckfield. Parking in layby opposite wood in Rocks Road. (TQ463217)
8 ha (20 acres)
Woodland Trust

A magical combination of water and trees gave Lake Wood its name and inspired generations of visitors.

In the 18th century the Streatfield family landscaped the site in the style of Capability Brown, creating a large lake and nearby water garden planted with exotic trees and shrubs.

Rocky sandstone outcrops, with high cliffs overhanging the water, add to the dramatic beauty. A tunnel cut through the rock completes the path around the lake which supports an interesting fish population and the impressive royal fern, rare elsewhere in Sussex.

The storms of 1987 created chaos but since the Woodland Trust took over a decade ago, much has been done to arrest an invasion of rhododendron.

Much of the wood is still ancient coppice supporting a wide variety of ancient woodland flowers and a fascinating wildlife population. Lake Wood is home to dormice and almost 60 species of bird – including kingfisher and heron.

MAP 2

Kiln Wood
Blackboys

B2192 south of Blackboys, turn
into Hollow Lane, entrance 400m
on left. (TQ522201)
13 ha (32 acres) AONB
Woodland Trust

Kiln Wood illustrates the need
to protect our precious
remnants of ancient woodland.

Look for bluebells, lords and
ladies, wood anemone and
garlic mustard – species which
indicate an area of ancient
woodland. These can be found
in one third of the site.
Adjoining this are two areas of
new native woodland planted to
help protect and extend this

rare and important habitat.
Look for a group of wild boar
made from willow.

While mostly easy going, the
land then gently slopes towards
a stream which runs from the
northeast diagonally through
the wood to exit adjacent to
the woodland entrance.

The high forest canopy is
dominated by mature oak with
lesser amounts of sycamore,
Norway maple, ash, alder and
other native species. Below you
will find a mixture of coppice,
bramble and young broadleaves
naturally regenerating.

Visitors can enjoy gentle walks
using a good network of tracks
and rides, which link well with
local public rights of way and
the adjoining landscape.

Gravetye
East Grinstead

From Turner's Hill, take the B2028
southeast for approximately 1.6km
(1 mile). Turn left towards
Sharpthorne, and left again into
Vowells Lane. Car park is on the
right, 400m (0.25 mile) beyond the
entrance to Gravetye Manor.
(TQ364351) 257 ha (635 acres)
Forestry Commission

The undulating landscape
beneath this large mixed
plantation provides contrasting
experiences as well as the
occasional challenge for visitors.

Where rides are made up the
walking is good while other
routes have become overgrown
and more suitable for the
adventurous who have come
dressed to explore.

One minute you could be
walking beneath huge columns

of western hemlock and Corsican pine then through a plantation of beech.

Owned by the William Robinson Charity, named after the gardener credited for the original planting and design of the Gravetye Manor estate, the site is popular with local visitors.

Follow the Sussex Border Path which meanders through the site. Before emerging on the eastern edge, where it continues via the shore of Weir Wood reservoir, you will have experienced the site in all its variety from dense plantation to open areas and a lake.

Friston Forest
Friston

Take the A259 west from Eastbourne. At the Seven Sisters Country Park at Exceat, take the minor road to Litlington on the right. The car park is on the right, 100m beyond the right turn to West Dean village. (TQ519001) 858 ha (2121 acres) AONB
Forestry Commission

Easy on the eye – and the walker's legs – Friston Forest is developing into a special section of the South Downs Area of Outstanding Natural Beauty.

Colourful in spring and autumn, this Forest Enterprise plantation is a massive 1920s forest that is dominated by beech. As the trees grow ▶▶

Friston Forest

MAP 2

and mature the site will increase in interest, though there are occasional large conifers to be seen along the ride edges.

Family visitors are well looked after. Information is available from nearby Seven Sisters Country Park where cycles are available for hire and good picnic facilities are provided near two spacious car parks.

Exploration is along gentle to moderate slopes and waymarked trails cater for cyclists and walkers who can tackle the one-and-a-half-hour White Horse View from the West Dean car park or the slightly shorter one-hour Butchers Trudge route from the Butchershole car park. There is even a Trim Trail for runners – especially devised for the energetic.

Moat Wood
East Hoathly, Uckfield

South of Uckfield on A22, two entrances off South Street, East Hoathly. (TQ516159)
10 ha (25 acres)
Woodland Trust

A classic example of Sussex ancient woodland, Moat Wood is particularly wonderful in May, with nightingales and other birds in full song.

Walk into the heart of the wood and you will discover a

Moat Wood

medieval moat, now a scheduled ancient monument, surrounding a square island of mixed coppice.

A network of paths and rides provides access through the wood, which is emerging as a real wildlife haven. As rides can become muddy after rain the wearing of boots is advised.

Once dominated by a dense canopy of tall oaks, it was hit by the storms of 1987. For the first time in many years some areas the woodland floor became open to sunlight. New planting and natural regeneration has brought benefits to wildlife.

Bluebells, wood anemone and an unusual proliferation of common cow-wheat are clues to the wood's great age, and there are signs of deer.

Stanmer Great Wood
Brighton

From the A27 east of Brighton, follow signs for Stanmer Park. The Great Wood is on the left of the park before the house.
(TQ343087)
60 ha (148 acres) AONB
Brighton and Hove Council

Lying on the slopes to the south and western edges of Stanmer Park, the woodland provides an attractive backdrop to the busy park below.

Once owned by the Earl of Chichester, the estate includes a 19th-century manor house (not open to the public) and park – the woods have been open to the public for over 50 years.

The transition from park to woodland is gradual with plenty of natural regeneration to soften the edges. Evidence of more formal planting can be seen in wonderful large planes, yew and cedar (near the house) as well as the occasional spreading oak and tall beech. Toward the northern edge at Chalk Hill young ash and sycamore are replacing the mature trees which fell in the storms of 1987.

Main rides, hugging the contours of the slopes, link to a maze of paths winding through the wood where views can be glimpsed over the park and toward Hollingbury Castle to the south.

MAP 3

- Tilbury
- Gravesend
- R Thames
- Sheerness
- Rochester
- Herne Bay
- Whitstable
- Shorne Wood Country Park p107
- Gillingham
- Saxten's & Cage's p106
- Chatham
- Sittingbourne
- Faversham
- Blean Wood p110
- Trosley Country Park p105
- Hucking Estate p108
- Canterbury
- Larkey Valley Wood p113
- Oldbury Hill p104
- Maidstone
- North
- Park Wood p116
- Denge Wood p115
- Sevenoaks
- Earley Wood p114
- Downs
- Kings Wood p117
- Tonbridge
- Dering Wood p120
- K E N T
- Ashford
- Packing & Soapers Wood p118
- Folkestone
- Tudeley Woods p98
- Bedgebury Pinetum p99
- Tunbridge Wells
- Hythe
- Friezland Wood p96
- Hargate Forest p98
- Scotney Castle Estate p100
- Cranbrook
- Hamstreet Woods p119
- Eridge Rocks p96
- Comfort's Wood p101
- Tenterden
- Nap Wood p95
- Crowborough
- New Romney
- Wilderness Wood p94
- Darch's Wood p93
- Flatropers Wood p103
- Heathfield
- Rye
- Selwyns Wood p92
- Dungeness
- E A S T   S U S S E X
- Battle
- Guestling Wood p102
- Park Wood p92
- Hailsham
- Abbots Wood p91
- Hastings
- Bexhill-on-Sea
- MAP 2 ▲ (see p46)
- Eastbourne
- Beachy Head
- 10 miles
- 10 km

90

Abbots Wood
Arlington

Take the A22 south from the Boship roundabout. Turn right on to minor road after approximately 3km (2 miles), then take the next left. The car park is on the left 400m (0.25 mile) beyond The Old Oak public house. (TQ556074) 356 ha (880 acres)

Forestry Commission

Wonderful spring bluebells are just one of the seasonal delights to discover in Abbots Wood.

The site, named during the reign of Henry I when it was given to Battle Abbey, has more ecclesiastical connections – the lake in its heart was created in medieval times by monks from nearby Michelham Priory.

But modern needs are not forgotten – picnic and barbecue facilities are provided, with a children's adventure playground near the car park.

Those keen to explore can choose from two waymarked circular trails – the one-hour Abbot's amble passes the lake, and the shorter Oak Walk takes in a variety of woodland types. Though these cover a relatively small portion of the site there are other forest tracks and paths to explore on generally level ground.

The wood, which also has some conifer plantations, supports dormice and a range of woodland butterflies – look out for pearl-bordered fritillaries.

MAP 3

Park Wood
Hellingly

From the A271, travelling east
from Upper Horsebridge, turn left
into Park Road (signed Hellingly
Hospital). 2.5km (1.5 miles)
towards Grove Hill, car park is on
right. (TQ603125)
60 ha (148 acres)
East Sussex County Council

Once part of Anderida, an
ancient forest that covered vast
areas of the south east, Park
Wood has a rich history.

The site once formed part of
a medieval deer park – hence
the name – and still has signs
of a ditch and bank system
along the boundary. There are
also remains of Canadian army
trenches from the Second
World War.

Visitors with less interest in
historic events can enjoy the
atmosphere of this oak-
dominated wood where wide
and sunny areas contrast with
denser, more shaded sections
and the walking is not
too taxing.

Spring is a good time to
enjoy displays of wood
anemone, bluebell, yellow
archangel and foxgloves while
fungi add autumn interest. You
might catch a glimpse of roe
deer or dormice.

A selection of circular
waymarked routes is provided,
including a good route for the
less able which meanders past a
pond and seating area.

Selwyns Wood
Heathfield or Hailsham

Enter Cross in Hand from
Heathfield. Take left turn in village
into Fir Grove Road. Take track on
left marked by Sussex Wildlife Trust
sign, next to house called White
Lodge (sign tricky to spot)
(TQ551205) 11 ha (27 acres) AONB
Sussex Wildlife Trust

Although this is an ancient
woodland site, past
management techniques have
resulted in the loss of many
'old wood' characteristics.

Remote and peaceful, this is a
good place to enjoy displays of
spring flowers. A stream
running through it has rare
mosses and liverworts
growing alongside.

A typical Wealdon mix, it is

made up of high forest with chestnut coppice and the additional interest of heathland areas.

The storms of 1987 damaged the site badly but this allowed the clearance of many conifer areas, which have been replanted with a more typical regional woodland mix – oak, wild cherry, hornbeam and hazel.

Woodpeckers and woodcock number among the bird population. The walking is generally easy along unmarked paths and tracks but is quite steep near the stream and the paths a little overgrown in places.

Darch's Wood
Heathfield

At Cross-in-Hand turn south into A267 Eastbourne Road. Shortly on right is St Bartholomew's Church and car park. Entrance to wood is behind church. (TQ569215)
16 ha (40 acres) AONB
Heathfield and Waldron Parish Council

Nestling in a pretty setting behind the church of St Bartholomew in Cross-in-Hand, Darch's Wood is an interesting blend of natural woodland and formal features.

The site, thought to be ancient woodland, is a typical East Sussex blend of oak, beech, birch, sweet chestnut and sallow near the paths, with ash in damper areas. A small number of larch have been planted and there is also an unusual, man-made causeway bounded by laurel hedge in the northwestern part of the site.

It's also worth looking out for a formalized pond/lake complex in the southern section which includes an interesting Japanese-style bridge.

The wood was hit by the storms of 1987 but areas have been cleared and planted with oak and regeneration is flourishing. And some large, impressive beech trees in the southern section hint at what it was like before 1987.

A stream runs from the north to the south of the wood, and there are paths of various types.

MAP 3

Wilderness Wood
Uckfield

On south side of A272 in Hadlow
Down village, 8km (5 miles)
northeast of Uckfield. Follow
brown tourist signs. (TQ536240)
23 ha (61 acres) AONB

Chris and Anne Yarrow

Award-winning Wilderness
Wood has it all – comprehensive
family facilities, events
programme, excellent
information and a rich wood
and wildlife mix.

Hailed for its people-friendly
approach and its commitment
to the environment alike,
Wilderness Wood is a family-
run working woodland that
offers a fully interpreted package
– but still allows you to 'get
away from it all'.

It is colourful in spring with
wood anemone and bluebells,
and again in autumn with a
display of fungi. Adding
atmosphere are lush mosses,
liverworts and ferns by the
stream.

A mile-long woodland trail
allows the visitor to experience
the different habitats. Most of
the woodland, which includes a
small heath, is dominated by
sweet chestnut coppice though a
few mature and ancient trees
survived the 1987 storms.
Winter visitors to the 6.5ha (16
acre) conifer plantation can even
cut their own Christmas trees.

Children are well catered for
and a separate trail is designed
for the less-able.

Wilderness Wood

Nap Wood
Frant

Take the A267 south from Tunbridge Wells. Nap Wood is about 3km (2 miles) south of Frant, on the left opposite a minor road turning to the right. Park on the verge. (TQ583327)
43 ha (107 acres) AONB SSSI
National Trust

Although parking facilities are limited, Nap Wood is well worth a visit if you're looking for a peaceful, unspoilt woodland walk.

An ancient woodland site, it stands on the edge of Eridge Old Park, reputedly one of England's oldest and largest deer parks – King John was said to have kept a hunting lodge at nearby Frant.

The sound of nearby traffic is left behind as you make your way through some fantastic, big old trees. Open areas afford views through the oak woodland, with large, mature standards, along with birch, rowan and the occasional massive beech.

In spring the woodland floor has carpets of bluebells and in autumn the bracken is beautiful bathed in dappled light.

There is a circular, if occasionally muddy, route along a gently sloping path which can by found by walking down the sunken track from the entrance gate, and bearing left.

Bluebells adding their spring colour

MAP 3

Eridge Rocks
Tunbridge Wells

Entrance is via a private road off
the A26 in Eridge Green between
the church and a small printing
works. (TQ554355)
40 ha (99 acres) AONB SSSI
Sussex Wildlife Trust

Impressive, even from the car
park, Eridge Rocks supports
ancient, almost gravity-defying
gnarled beech, yew and hollies
which thrive on an ancient
sandstone outcrop dating back
135 million years.

Massive sandstone boulders
stand out among the mixed
woodland and support 150
types of plant – little wonder
this site is designated of Special
Scientific Interest.

There are plans to improve
the already good path network
which meanders through this
quiet and peaceful site.

The woods are a mixture of
chestnut coppice and oak with
a display of bluebells in spring.
Alder trees line the woodland
stream and there is a good
array of birds including tits,
nuthatches and woodpeckers.

The spread of rhododendron,
planted by the Victorians, was
crowding out locally distinctive
plants so Sussex Wildlife Trust
is removing much of it. As a
result, mosses, liverworts and
ferns are now thriving.

Adjoining is Broadwater
Wood, a Scots pine plantation
with beech, birch and oak on
the fringes.

Friezland Wood
Tunbridge Wells

Follow High Rocks Lane east out
of Tunbridge Wells. (TQ562383)
8 ha (20 acres) AONB SSSI
Woodland Trust

Small but packed with interest,
Friezland Wood on the
Kent–East Sussex border is
something of a British rarity,
thanks to the unusual rock
formations on its western side.

Rising out of the highest
cliffs of the Weald, the Ardingly
sandstone rock formations are
so unusual they have earned
part of the site SSSI status and
nurtured a rich mixture of
lichens, ferns and bryophytes.

Set on a steep north-facing
slope, the site has three distinct

Friezland Wood

sections: its upper slopes feature oak, ash, alder and birch with an abundance of wood anemones, bluebells and some bramble. The vertical rocks support yew, sessile oak and holly, with a flatter area where alder, with nettles, buttercups and celandines grow.

Popular with local people, Friezland has a good network of paths though some can get muddy and waterlogged in winter.

The remains of a hill fort, dating back to 150–50BC survives a short distance from the southwest boundary of this ancient woodland.

MAP 3

Hargate Forest
Tunbridge Wells

Entrance off Broadwater Down,
just off A26. (TQ574370)
61 ha (151 acres)
Woodland Trust

Set just south of Tunbridge
Wells is big, broad and
beautiful Hargate Forest –
perfect for those 'getting away
to the country'.

Part of the heavily wooded
High Weald, the mixed
woodland supports an
abundance of butterflies not
often found in the region and
a rich bird population. It is
popular with people too!

Hargate has a good track, ride
and path network where you
can complete a circular walk,
but some sections can get
muddy.

Set on sloping land, there are
extensive views from the
regenerating heathland areas
and a brook flows through its
southern section. The
Woodland Trust has created
ponds throughout the site.

The old forest, in the south,
has the real feel of ancient
woodland and boasts some fine
old beech trees. Look out for
lily-of-the-valley – rare in the
area.

Work is ongoing to thin
conifers and control
rhododendron, encouraging
the regeneration of native trees
and boosting biodiversity.

Tudeley Woods
Tonbridge

Take the A21 south from
Tonbridge. After 1.6km (1 mile)
take minor road to Capel, turning
left before Shell garage. Car park is
800m (0.5 mile) on the left.
(TQ616433)
287 ha (709 acres)
RSPB

One of the largest areas of
ancient woodland in the
southeast, Tudeley Woods is a
haven for birdlife.

Using traditional techniques
such as coppicing and charcoal
burning, the RSPB is
maintaining a thriving wildlife
habitat.

This is particularly evident in
spring with wonderful shows
of bluebells and primroses, and

the woods are alive with birdsong from a host of warblers breeding here.

The oak woodland supports nuthatches, three woodpecker species and tawny owls, while the adjacent meadow is important for willow warblers, whitethroats and yellow hammers and for goldfinches, redpolls and siskins in autumn.

Summer visitors can enjoy the sights and smells of a variety of orchids and a host of colourful butterflies.

Two waymarked trails take the explorer through areas of light and shade, providing good views over the Kent countryside. Some paths are quite steep and potentially slippery.

Bedgebury Pinetum
Goudhurst

Take the A21 north from Flimwell and after about 1.6 km (1 mile) turn right onto the B2079 to Goudhurst. (TQ715388)
120 ha (297 acres) AONB
Forestry Commission

Hailed as one of the world's finest conifer collections, Bedgebury Pinetum boasts a beautiful plantation of 6,000 impressive trees set beside landscaped lakes and valleys.

Located in an area of outstanding natural beauty, this peaceful scene contains some of Britain's oldest and largest conifers including rare, endangered and historically important trees. They are set

around a fabulous lake complete with pretty bridge, beautiful lilies and enchanting reflections.

Founded by the Forestry Commission and Kew Gardens in the 1920s, visitors can enjoy year-round interest: rhododendrons and azaleas in spring; shaded glades, lakes and stream in summer; autumn colour with fungi, fruits and berries and a Christmas card landscape in winter.

Follow the waymarked Trees of the World route or a choice of two trails in the neighbouring forest. A programme of walks, talks and events, creative play areas plus a new visitor centre with bike hire, ensures adults and children are well catered for.

MAP 3

Scotney Castle Estate

Scotney Castle Estate
Lamberhurst

2.5km (1.5 miles) south of
Lamberhurst, on the east of the
A21, 13km (8 miles) southeast of
Tunbridge Wells. (TQ688353)
311 ha (770 acres)
National Trust

Scotney Castle Estate is
beautiful to explore and has a
variety of woods to visit.

Stately, old lichen-clad trees
dot the open parkland areas.
Woodland ranges from ancient
trees in Kilndown Wood to
mixed broadleaves in High
Forest and stands of coppiced
sweet chestnut in Collier's
Wood.

A garden and shop are open
from late March to early
November but visitors are
advised to check on opening
times in advance.

A four-mile waymarked trail leads through mixed woodland – some of it ancient – taking in parkland, meadow and the River Bewl with good views across the estate and parkland to the old ruined castle. Look for oast houses, hop gardens, hoppers' huts and ponds – signs that brewing was once an important part of the local economy.

There are other short, occasionally rough and muddy routes to follow so remember those sturdy boots.

Comfort's Wood
Cranbrook

Take the B2086 from the A229 and head east towards Beneden. Wood is adjacent to Swattenden Lane (B2086) and entrance is opposite the Swattenden Centre. (TQ771346)

11 ha (27 acres) AONB

Woodland Trust

Comfort's Wood, half a mile south of Cranbrook village in the High Weald AONB, takes its name from the couple who gifted the site to the Woodland Trust in 1990.

Since then the Trust has worked to develop the commercial orchard and arable land that made up the site, with a programme of planting.

The site is bordered to the north by a belt of mature oak-dominated broadleaved woodland, a small narrow section of which extends into Comfort. Exploration of these older trees leads to a small seasonal stream where bluebells and wood anemones burst into life each spring.

Grassy glades and rides form a circular path around the edges of the site, linking with a broad ride which allows access right through the middle of the wood. In the northwest corner is a small seasonal pond surrounded by bushes and shrubs.

MAP 3

Guestling Wood

Guestling Wood
Hastings
Car park situated in Watermill
Lane between Pett and Icklesham.
(TQ861147)
45 ha (111 acres)
Woodland Trust

Spring brings the promise of
spectacular wood anemone and
bluebell displays in Guestling
Wood, a typical High Weald
ancient woodland.

The Woodland Trust owns
around half of the sweet
chestnut-dominated site.
Guestling's rich ground flora is
being encouraged through a
programme of coppicing,
particularly in the northern
part of the wood.

Two public footpaths and a
good network of rides and
paths link the site with the
surrounding countryside and
lead the visitor through
frequent scene changes.

The eastern side sits on top
of a ridge which falls away to
the west. A small stream,
known as Lady Brook, flows
along the site's western
boundary.

In contrast, the lower section
of the wood is much wetter,
with different ground and tree
cover. Edging the stream are
willow, alder and ash with
clumps of sedge and rush at
their base. Further south, the
chestnut makes way for hazel
coppice while oak standards
dot the entire site.

Flatropers Wood

Flatropers Wood
Rye

Entrance is on the east side of
Bixley Lane, which leaves the A268
on the south side of a sharp bend
south of Beckley. (TQ861231)
35 ha (87 acres) AONB
Sussex Wildlife Trust

Birdsong is all that is likely to
break the peace on a walk
through remote Flatropers
Wood, a mixed ancient
woodland in a quiet corner
of Sussex.

Although surrounded by
conifer plantations, the unspoilt
mixture of oak, hornbeam,
hazel and occasional pine
plantation provides a delightful
variety of wildlife habitats.

It takes between one and two
hours to tour the reserve over
generally gentle terrain that can
get muddy underfoot in winter.

Inside the wood are areas of
large oaks, and patches of
cleared birch where heather and
other heathland plants support
lizards and insects such as the
rare green tiger beetle.

Coppicing has created sunny
spots where spring flowers burst
into life, supporting a variety of
butterflies. Interest is added by a
stream and small pond on the
eastern side of the wood.

Wild boar hoofprints are
occasionally spotted on the
paths, though the animals
themselves are a much
rarer sight.

MAP 3

Oldbury Hill

Oldbury Hill
Sevenoaks

On the north side of the A25, 5km
(3 miles) southwest of Wrotham.
(TQ582561)
62 ha (153 acres) AONB SSSI
National Trust

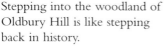

Stepping into the woodland of
Oldbury Hill is like stepping
back in history.

This is the site of an Iron Age
fortress with massive ramparts –
one of them is a mammoth 2.5
miles long. Built in 100–50BC
by the Wealden Celts, it is one
of our largest hillforts whose
gateways controlled an
important crossing of the River
Medway.

As you walk beneath the huge
beeches that grow on the
ramparts today, or along the
route of the prehistoric track
that crosses the site – it is not
difficult to conjure up
characters from the past.

Parts of the mixed woodland
– oak, birch, rowan, beech and
some Scots pine – have
probably been coppiced since
Saxon times.

Visitors can view the site from
two steep waymarked trails
taking in the dappled shade of
open woodland – one of 1.6km
(1 mile) and the other
stretching for 5km (3 miles).

Trosley Country Park
Meopham

From the A227 follow signs to Vigo Village. Turn right into Waterlow Road and park is opposite. (TQ634612) 69 ha (170 acres)

Kent County Council

Natural without being wild and well laid out without being over-interpreted, Trosley Country Park on the crest of the North Downs is a great place to 'get out into the countryside'.

Two main routes serve the woodland, which boasts a wonderful bluebell display in the spring and provide fantastic views across the Weald. The red route runs via a long straight path cut into the side of the hill, where overhanging trees create a striking tunnel effect. En route are seats and sculptures and some large, impressive yew trees.

The blue route is a steep, hilly path across chalk downland where Exmoor ponies graze and the show of wildflowers in spring and summer adds colour.

Wildlife thrives here with red admiral, speckled wood and common blues among the butterfly population. Rare species such as the chalkhill blue and green fritillary live on the chalk grassland. Birds include woodpecker, kestrel, hawfinch and treecreeper.

MAP 3

Saxten's & Cage's
Fawkham Green

From Farningham take A20 towards West Kingsdown and after 2.5km (1.5 miles) turn left, signposted Fawkham Green. Opposite Brand's Hatch circuit turn left for Fawkham Green going underneath M20 and turn right immediately into Roger's Wood Lane. Continue up a short hill, main entrance on left at the top of hill. (TQ586649) 23 ha (57 acres)
Woodland Trust

Just 800m from the roar of Brand's Hatch, on the sides and plateau of a beautiful valley, stands Saxten's and Cage's Wood – a valued and well-loved piece of the Kent landscape.

Once managed as two woods but now treated as a single entity with two distinctive characters, the site has a wide range of species, including those typical of ancient woodland. It is important for its wildlife, particularly dormice. In fact, it has Class II status for nature conservation importance.

Parts of the site resemble tangled jungle – the result of damage cause by the devastating storms of 1987. Many of the trees that fell were left and now form valuable habitats, though some of the rides were blocked, hampering free access to sections of the site.

However walkers and ramblers make good use of the public footpath that bisects the woodland and the interesting routes around and through most of it.

Dormouse

Shorne Wood Country Park

Shorne

Adjacent to the A2, between Gravesend and Rochester. Take Shorne/Cobham turning. Country Park is signposted from A2 with brown signs. (TQ684699)

70 ha (174 acres) SSSI

Kent County Council

There is plenty to keep visitors happy at Shorne Wood Country Park, a site well served with good facilities and delightful ancient woodland.

A mixture of heathland, wetland, meadows and woodland, Shorne Wood caters for everyone with a 3km horse and cycle route, fishing lake, sensory garden and even a dog swimming pond!

There is a real country park feel to the area surrounding the car park and visitor centre so many people might never be tempted to stray far. There is a busy events programme, children's adventure playground and a 'Wood Henge' seating feature as well as a range of woodland sculptures carved from fallen chestnut. An excellent arboretum in the centre of the car park is planted with clearly labelled native trees – excellent for woodland 'novices'.

Follow the purple or red trails to discover 'real' woodland with some large trees, including birch, sweet chestnut, oak sycamore and beech.

MAP 3

Hucking Estate
Hollingbourne

From A20 roundabout near Leeds Castle take B2163 through Hollingbourne heading towards Sittingbourne. At top of hill at small crossroads turn left towards Hucking. Follow for 2.5km (1.5 miles) and turn left at road junction signposted Hucking. Car park 100m on left. (TQ843575) 235 ha (581 acres)
Woodland Trust

Five miles north of Maidstone, in Kent's Downs Area of Outstanding Natural Beauty, is the Hucking Estate, a 232-hectare mix of farmland and woods with a wealth of archaeological 'gems'.

A series of paths, including two waymarked trails, guide visitors through areas of coppiced ash, sweet chestnut, sycamore and hornbeam, passing fine examples of mature beech and oak toward new woodland-creation schemes. An extensive planting programme sees 78 hectares of new broadleaved woodland being created.

Clearance work has opened up darker areas, creating wide rides and allowing light to reach the woodland floor, stimulating development of butterfly-attracting flora. The main shrub species include hawthorn, elder and hazel, while bluebells dominate the ground cover along with dog's mercury, wood anemone, red campion and foxglove and are most conspicuous during the spring and summer months.

Archaeology enthusiasts can examine a host of interesting features, including an ancient drove road, woodbank and marl pits.

MAP 3

Blean Wood
Canterbury

Situated between the A2 and A290. From A2 take exit signposted
Canterbury and left signposted Rough Common. At north end of Rough
Common, small brown sign on left indicates Blean NNR. Follow stoned
track into wood to car park, 300 metres. (TR102593)
530 ha (1310 acres) SSSI
Various

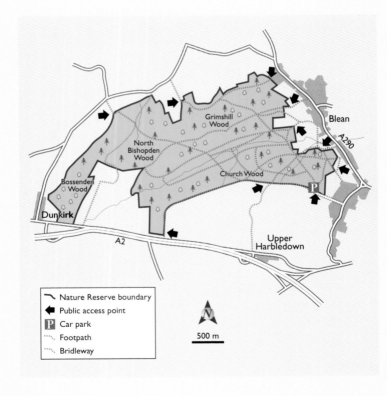

Blean Wood

The Blean, Kent's second most extensive concentration of woodland, is one of the largest broadleaved nature reserves in Britain. The Woodland Trust, English Nature and the RSPB manage the Blean National Nature Reserve (NNR) as a partnership.

The Blean makes up the northwestern half of a great ring of woods surrounding Canterbury. Despite its vast size visitors still find these woods intimate and constant habitat changes keep your interest alive.

The area is managed to protect its valuable mosaic of habitats which vary from sunny glades and heathland to ancient woodland, areas of coppice and conifer plantation, much of which is being thinned and nurtured back to native broadleaves.

Easy enough to reach from minor roads and tracks, the woodlands of the Blean remain relatively remote though they have seen many changes over the centuries.

The area's mature woodland boasts some large oak with, less frequently, beech and decaying trees that help sustain a vast array of wildlife. Some 29 species of butterfly have been recorded here as well as an impressive number of woodland birds, dormice and ants, which thrive in huge wood nests.

In spring some of the woods are positively idyllic, with fine

MAP 3

floral displays of bluebell, wood anemone, primrose, violet and ladies smock edging the paths.

From the car park, four colour-coded waymarked trails range from just a mile to more than seven. Dog owners have their own route, and there are many other rides and tracks to explore. Generally flat, they vary in shape and size from meandering path to wide forest tracks. Growing along some rides is the less-than-common, common cow-wheat, an essential food plant for the rare heath fritillary butterfly.

Close to the car park is a picnic area with interactive sculptures – a man-made addition to the Blean's more natural features.

To commemorate the 200th anniversary of the Battle of Trafalgar, local residents and children from nearby schools are helping the Woodland Trust create Victory Wood on the Blean's northwest boundary.

Hornbeam

Larkey Valley Wood
Canterbury

Take A28 from Canterbury
towards Ashford and first left into
St Nicholas Road after crossing
over A2 and follow road round to
right into Cockering Road. Car
park is 1.6km (1 mile) on the left.
(TR124557)
43 ha (106 acres) SSSI
Canterbury City Council

Spring is probably the best
time to enjoy Larkey Valley
Wood, when it is filled with a
mass of flowers, the star of
which is the rare lady orchid,
one of eight orchid species
growing here.

This is an ancient woodland
site, with a wide variety of
trees and shrubs. To identify
the soil under your feet look
for beech and hazel which
grow on chalky soil while oak,
hornbeam and sweet chestnut
enjoy areas of more acidic clay
with flints.

There is an extensive path
network and two waymarked
routes. Paths can be narrow
and slippery in the wet.

The storms of 1987 have left
their mark with dense thickets
taking over parts of the south
and eastern edge though some
clearance work has been
undertaken. The traditional
practice of coppicing can still
be seen in parts of the wood.

From the car park, views
extend over the Great Stour
valley and surrounding
countryside.

MAP 3

Earley Wood
Petham

Situated between Petham and
Waltham approimately 8.5km (5.5
miles) southwest of Canterbury.
From Petham village take road
southwest signposted Waltham.
After about 1km (0.75 mile) Earley
Wood and car park spaces are on
the left. (TR120502)
22 ha (54 acres) AONB

Woodland Trust

Mystery surrounds the origins
of Earley Wood, but the heart of
the site is thought to be ancient
woodland.

Five miles southwest of
Canterbury, the wood forms
part of the North Kent Downs
Area of Outstanding Natural
Beauty and offers views over
countryside to the south.

It is a rich mix of coppiced
broadleaved woodland with oak,
ash, beech, chestnut and
occasional sycamore.

A splendid beech and
hornbeam avenue that used to
stand in the heart of the wood
was damaged in the 1987 storm.

Around 110 different
woodland plant species,
including small colonies of herb
paris, a wonderful collection of
orchids and swathes of bluebells
that clothe the woodland floor
in spring.

Badgers and birds thrive on
the site with dark bush crickets
and speckled bush crickets being
two of the many rare
invertebrates recorded here.
Watch out, too, for adders in the
area formerly called Deadley's
Wood.

Earley Wood

Denge Wood
Garlinge Green, Chartham

From A28 turn off to Shalmsford Street and, reaching the eastern end of the village, turn right into Mystole Lane and right again after 1km (0.5 mile) into Penny Pot Lane. After 1.6km (1 mile) the road enters Denge wood with car parking space on the left. (TR104523)
26 ha (64 acres) AONB
Woodland Trust

Dating back to at least 1600, Denge Wood is part of a semi-natural ancient wood complex on the North Downs, a few miles southwest of Canterbury.

Dominated by sweet chestnut coppice, it stands alongside an area of former chalk grassland, known as The Warren. This combination provides an interesting wildlife habitat, which is ideal for, among other species, the rare Duke of Burgundy fritillary butterfly.

The Woodland Trust is keen to build on the wood's biodiversity and the creation of a wide ride has expanded the invertebrate habitat. A small population of deer can also occasionally be seen.

Because the land is clay over chalk bedrock, the wood can get wet and muddy in winter. But venturing within unveils two gently sloping dry valleys running northeast to southwest through the wood.

Denge is crossed by two footpaths and accessed via a small, informal car park from Pennypot Lane.

Denge Wood

MAP 3

Park Wood
Chilham
2.5km (1.5 miles) southwest of
Chilham, adjacent to A252.
(TR042526)
23 ha (57 acres) AONB SSSI
Woodland Trust

Visitors to this ancient
woodland can enjoy a wood of
two distinctive halves.

On the western side you can
stroll beneath a mixed canopy
of fine old sweet chestnuts and
oaks with coppiced hornbeam
beneath. By contrast, to the
east of the main gateway is
more dense cover including
hazel and hawthorn.

Within the coppiced areas
there are also many old
pollarded hornbeam trees.
These were frequently used by
woodcutters to mark the
boundary of coppiced areas.

The site can be explored via
two good circular paths which
lead through the wood from
inside the main gateway. The
paths are edged with a
wonderful collection of
flowering plants which are
particularly good for
butterflies. To maintain this
important habitat, the Trust
regularly coppices edges of the
path network.

The terrain is gently
undulating but there are short
sections which can be steep
and slippery in winter.

Hazelnuts

Kings Wood
Ashford

Take the A28 to Canterbury from Ashford. Approx 5km (3 miles) out of Ashford turn left towards Challock. Car park is 2.5km (1.5 miles) on the right. (TR025500) 574 ha (1419 acres) AONB

Forestry Commission

Autumn is one of the best times to visit, when Kings Wood is full of colour and sweet chestnuts can be harvested.

The woods are best viewed by taking the Beech Walk, a three-mile trail, where children can delight in discovering sculptures created by local artists.

Varied paths lead visitors through closed canopies and open spaces. As well as conifers, which are the dominant feature, pockets of ancient woodland survive with yew and hornbeam and coppiced areas of beech as well as sweet chestnut.

Bluebell and lady orchid are among the many beautiful floral species that thrive here. Bird sightings include goldcrest, nightingale and three species of woodpecker.

Close to the car park is a picnic area with play sculptures, while older visitors appreciate views from the open area nearby.

Boots are always a good idea, since it can get muddy.

117

MAP 3

Packing Wood
Hamstreet

Situated 1.6km (1 mile) north of
Hamstreet on the west of A2070
bypass. However, access is not
advised off the A2070. Take road
through Hamstreet heading north
towards Bromley Green. After
A2070 turning take second right at
staggered crossroads into Capel
Lane. Entrance on right after
approximately 1km (0.75 mile).
(TR005352)
41 ha (101 acres) SSSI
Woodland Trust

Packing Wood, part of the
much larger Hamstreet Woods
Site of Special Scientific
Interest, is renowned for its
outstanding invertebrate and
breeding woodland bird
populations.

Nationally important species
– like the silver-washed
fritillary and grizzled skipper
butterflies – thrive here.

A variety of tree species can
be found, including sweet
chestnut and conifers, which
make up more than two thirds
of the site, though work is
going on to gradually remove
these.

The rest is made up of open
spaces and areas of young,
developing oak and hornbeam
woodland.

There are several old wild
service trees among oak
hornbeam areas on the site,
along with one old wild pear
tree. Recent planting has
focused on native species such
as oak and wild cherry, along
with more exotic southern
beech and Norway maple.

The site is mainly flat and
includes a small damp gill
valley at its southeast corner. A
stream flows south through the
wood towards the valley.

Hamstreet Woods
Ashford, Kent

Turn off A2070 Ashford to Brenzett road into centre of Hamstreet. Follow one way system at crossroads to Dukes Head PH. Turn L at pillarbox just before Bournewood Stores. Continue to end of this no-through road to car park and main entrance.
(TR011341)
97 ha (240 acres) SSSI
English Nature

Hamstreet Woods, the 'star' site among a large complex of woods descended from a post-Ice Age forest, is nationally renowned for birds and moths.

Rare moths with such descriptive names as silky wave, merveille-du-jour, light orange underwing and the triangle populate this traditionally managed site. The site is of interest from the first shoots of spring to the autumn, when it is swathed in rich colour.

More than 30 trees and shrubs are found here. Oak and hornbeam thrive alongside wood anemone, bluebells and the occasional wild service tree in higher parts of the wood. In the damp valleys you'll discover ash, hazel and alder rising from a woodland floor covered with dog's mercury and orchids such as the greater butterfly and early purple.

Sited on the edge of a sandstone and clay plateau and sliced by a number of small valleys, the site can be explored by following three waymarked trails of varying lengths.

MAP 3

Dering Wood

Dering Wood
Pluckley

From A20 at Charing take road
signposted Pluckley and Smarden.
400m (0.25 mile) after Pluckley
turn right on road beside pub.
After 2.5km (1.5 miles) the road
passes between woodland. Dering
Wood car park is on the left.
(TQ900441) 125 ha (310 acres)
Woodland Trust

Saved from development,
Dering Wood can now
continue to support its vast
array of plant and wildlife that
is recognised for its
conservation interest.

The wood is home to many
species of butterfly and rare
beetles, and also renowned for
its stunning display of spring
bluebells and wood anemones.

Mostly ancient woodland, the
site features in records
stretching back 1,000 years.
Archaeological evidence can be
spotted in the shape of
drainage ditches, ponds, saw
pits and even the site of a
plane crash.

Oak and hornbeam coppice
covers much of Dering, a
distinctive feature of the
southeast. While there are
areas of high forest and dense
scrubby woodland, mature
coppice dominates.

Typical of Weald woodlands,
it can get very wet and muddy
underfoot in winter but it is
well served with access tracks.

WOODLAND
TRUST

Trees and forests are crucial to life on our planet. They generate oxygen, play host to a spectacular variety of wildlife and provide us with raw materials and shelter. They offer us tranquillity, inspire us and refresh our souls.

Founded in 1972, the Woodland Trust is now the UK's leading woodland conservation charity. By acquiring sites and campaigning for woodland it aims to conserve, restore and re-establish native woodland to its former glory. The Trust now owns and cares for over 1,100 woods throughout the UK.

The Woodland Trust wants to see:
no further loss of ancient woodland
the variety of woodland wildlife restored and improved
an increase in new native woodland
an increase in people's understanding and enjoyment of woodland

The Woodland Trust has 150,000 members who share this vision. For every new member, the Trust can care for approximately half an acre of native woodland. For details of how to join the Woodland Trust please either ring FREEPHONE 0800 026 9650 or visit the website at www.woodland-trust.org.uk.

If you have enjoyed the woods in this book please consider leaving a legacy to the Woodland Trust. Legacies of all sizes play an invaluable role in helping the Trust to create new woodland and secure precious ancient woodland threatened by development and destruction. For further information please either call 01476 581129 or visit our dedicated website at www.legacies.org.uk

The Chase

Further Information

Public transport

Each entry gives a brief description of location, nearest town and grid reference. Traveline provides impartial journey planning information about all public transport services either by ringing 0870 608 2608 (calls charged at national rates) or by visiting www.traveline.org.uk. For information about the Sustrans National Cycle Network either ring 0117 929 0888 or visit www.sustrans.org.uk

Useful contacts

Forestry Commission, 0845 367 3787, www.forestry.gov.uk
National Trust, 0870 458 4000, www.nationaltrust.org.uk
Wildlife Trusts, 0870 036 7711, www.wildlifetrusts.org
RSPB, 01767 680551, www.rspb.org.uk
Royal Forestry Society, 01442 822028, www.rfs.org.uk
National Community Forest Partnership, 01684 311880, www.communityforest.org.uk
Tree Council, 020 7407 9992, www.treecouncil.org.uk
Woodland Trust, 01476 581111, www.woodland-trust.org.uk

Recommend a Wood

You can play a part in helping us complete this series. We are inviting readers to nominate a wood or woods they think should be included. We are interested in any woodland with public access in England, Scotland, Wales and Northern Ireland.

To recommend a wood please photocopy this page and provide as much of the following information as possible:

About the wood

Name of wood: _____

Nearest town: _____

Approximate size: _____ ha/acres

Owner/manager: _____

A few words on why you think it should be included:

_____

_____

About you

Your name: _____

Your postal address: _____

_____

_____ Post code: _____

If you are a member of the Woodland Trust please provide your membership number.

Please send to: Exploring Woodland Guides, The Woodland Trust, Autumn Park, Dysart Road, Grantham, Lincolnshire NG31 6LL, by fax on 01476 590808 or e-mail woodlandguides@woodland-trust.org.uk

Thank you for your help

Other Guides in the Series

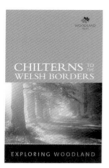

Chilterns to the
Welsh Borders

The South West
of England

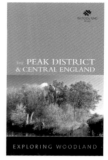

The Peak District
& Central England

Wales

Coming soon

East Anglia & North London

Scotland

Yorkshire & the North East

If you would like to be notified when certain titles are due for
publication please either write to Exploring Woodland Guides,
The Woodland Trust, Autumn Park, Dysart Road, Grantham,
Lincolnshire NG31 6LL or e-mail woodlandguides@woodland-
trust.org.uk

Index

Legal & General is delighted to support the Woodland Trust's conservation programme across the UK.

As a leading UK company, Legal & General recognises the importance of maintaining and improving our environment for future generations. We actively demonstrate our commitment through good management and support of environmental initiatives and organisations, such as the Woodland Trust.

Information on how Legal & General manages its impact on the environment can be found at www.legalandgeneralgroup.com/csr.